STARS OF TODAY
LEGENDS OF TOMORROW

STARS O

LEGENDS OF

This is a SEVENOAKS book

Copyright © Sevenoaks Ltd, 1999

First published by Sevenoaks Ltd, 1999

10 9 8 7 6 5 4 3 2 1

A CIP catalogue record for this book is available from the British Library

ISBN 1 85868 844 2

Project editors: Roland Hall and Chris Hawkes
Project art direction: Trevor Newman
Picture research: Lorna Ainger
Production: Sarah Schuman
Design: Simon Mercer

Printed and bound in Italy

This independent publication is the property of Sevenoaks Ltd and has been prepared without any involvement on the part of the National Basketball Association.

F TODAY

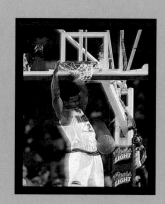

TOMORROW

Ben Osborne

SEVENOAKS

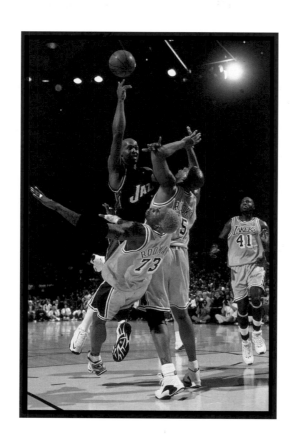

CONTENTS

MICHAEL JORDAN

TRIBUTE TO A LEGEND

Michael Jordan should be looked at as basketball's great Creator. Without him, it's unlikely that children throughout Europe would be running around in NBA jerseys or that Kevin Garnett would be making $21 million per year. Jordan is the single most prominent figure in NBA history, with a sphere of influence that includes every player, coach, referee and owner in the League — not to mention the millions of people around the world who strive to "Be Like Mike", despite never having met the man.

And while Jordan's good looks and charm did wonders for his marketability, it all started on the basketball court. Jordan's recently concluded career consisted of one highlight after another, from College Titles to Olympic Gold Medals, Slam Dunk Championships to collecting NBA Title rings.

Had Jordan stayed out of the game following his first retirement in 1993, fresh on the heels of his Bulls' third straight championship, he would already have been considered one of the greatest players to ever lace up a pair of sneaks. But when he came back and won three more from 1996–98 and further entrenched himself as the planet's most-recognizable face, Jordan moved onto a plane that no NBA athlete has ever reached, nor ever will.

Spoken superlatives about Jordan are even more numerous than all his accomplishments, but it was the normally stoic Larry Bird who captured Jordan's essence better than anyone else when he said, "I think he's actually God disguised as Michael Jordan."

Amen.

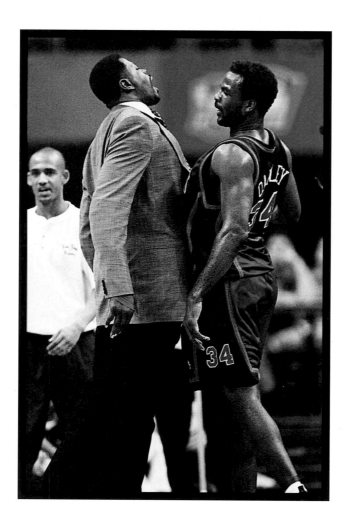

INTRODUCTION

THE TOP 100

A list of 100 of the NBA's top players is quite a disparate list. There's glitzy young players and grizzled veterans, sky-walking guards and earth-moving centers. One of the most amazing things about the NBA is that, out of its 350 or so players, very few of them have much in common. Nearly every single player has his own unique skills and personality, and by playing on a tiny court with no equipment on their bodies, NBA players have become a new breed of celebrity, each of whom bring their own special skills to the table. There is, of course, one big similarity between all NBA players, and that's in the paychecks, which usually have more zeros than most working stiffs see in their lifetime.

The following is a list of 100 of the League's richest, most compelling figures, including looks at all types of members of the·NBA's elite fraternity. What did Shaquille O'Neal make last season? Where did David Robinson go to college? How many points per game has Allen Iverson averaged in his young career? What do people have to say about Mark Jackson? The answers to all these questions are answered in this list of players who are seeking to make sure people still "Love this Game" — even after Michael Jordan has left it for good.

KEVIN GARNETT
Minnesota Timberwolves

$21,000,000 | **1**

Known as "The Man Who Changed The NBA" because of his tremendous six-year, $126 million contract, Kevin Garnett became in many people's minds the final reason for the 1998 NBA lockout. How did this unassuming young player, who jumped straight from high school to the NBA, end up as the league's top earner? With a devastating combination of on-court skills and an effervescent personality, that's how.

Even with a contract that many older observers begrudge, Garnett remains a fan favorite because of his amazing dunks, gangsta-slapping blocks, one-handed rebounds and no-look passes, all of which he executes with a wide grin on his face. And if KG's abilities don't capture the imaginations of fans and executives throughout the league, then the fact that he's already played four seasons and has only just turned 23 years old surely does. "He's still learning the game," says Timberwolves general manager (and former Celtic great) Kevin McHale. "It's hard to say that a player as good as he is has an upside to get a lot better, but he has it. Two or three years from now, he could be the top player in the game." Imagine that.

Stat Attack

Born:	May 19, 1976, Mauldin, SC
Ht/Wt:	7—0, 225 pounds
School:	Farragut HS (Chicago, IL)
Pro Career:	Minnesota Timberwolves (1995–)
Career Avgs:	16.2 ppg, 8.4 rpg, 3.3 apg

Career Highlights

1995	Selected with the fifth pick in the NBA Draft despite never playing a game of college basketball
1996	Named to the NBA All-Rookie second team
1997	Named to his first All-Star team
1998	Became the first All-Star starter in Timberwolves' history at New York's Madison Square Garden
1999	Led the Timberwolves to their third straight Playoff appearance (the only ones in franchise history)
1999	Selected for the USA basketball men's senior team for the 2000 Olympics

PATRICK EWING
New York Knicks

$17,000,000 | 2

A true on-court warrior, Patrick Ewing has been a part of more NBA battles than the rest of his teammates combined; and while he has yet to pick up a championship ring for his efforts, Ewing is still revered as a classic professional. In 1997 Ewing was lauded as one of the 50 Greatest Players in NBA History, an honor he earned by scoring, rebounding and blocking shots with proficiency throughout the late '80s and the entire '90s. His points have been accumulated with the help of a deadly 15- to 20-foot jumper that Ewing shoots better than any big man in NBA history.

Having completed his 14th season as a Knickerbocker – the longest tenure in franchise history – many expect Ewing to hang it up soon. But with two years left and a passion that still burns, PE ain't going anywhere.

"Patrick Ewing is an unbelievable player," says Larry Bird, former rival player and now head coach of the Knicks' nemesis, the Indiana Pacers. "Patrick comes to play every single game. When you start looking at guys with big hearts, he's definitely got one." Bird should know – Ewing's been teaching the NBA about heart for a long time now.

Stat Attack

Born:	August 5, 1962, Kingston, Jamaica
Ht/Wt:	7—0, 255 pounds
School:	Georgetown University
Pro Career:	New York Knicks (1985–)
Career Avgs:	23.3 ppg, 10.4 rpg, 2.1 apg

Career Highlights

1984	Won Olympic gold medal as collegian
1984	Won National Championship as a junior at Georgetown, also winning MVP
1985	Consensus choice as National Collegiate Player of the Year after senior season
1985	Selected with first overall pick of the NBA Draft
1986	Named NBA Rookie of the Year
1990	Named to NBA All-Star team as a starter for the first time
1992	Won his second Olympic gold medal as a member of the "Dream Team"
1993	Became Knicks' all-time leading scorer
1994	Finished fifth in League MVP voting as he helped Knicks to the NBA Finals for the first time in 21 years
1997	Scored 20,000th career point

SHAQUILLE O'NEAL
Los Angeles Lakers

$15,000,000   3

Shaquille O'Neal is, quite simply, the NBA's most dominant force. A monster of a man, Shaq has been barreling over defenders ever since he stepped on the court at Louisiana State University in 1989. Since entering the league as one of the most ballyhooed draft picks in history, "The Diesel" has delivered more face jobs to helpless opponents than one could count. And oh yeah — he's won tons of games as well. In just his third NBA season, O'Neal led the neophyte Orlando Magic past Michael Jordan's Chicago Bulls and into the NBA Finals; and after signing with the Lakers in 1996 for what was at the time the biggest contract in NBA history, Shaq instantly made Los Angeles a team to be reckoned with.

"Shaq is simply impossible to stop," says ex-Sonic and current Bucks coach George Karl. "The only thing you can hope for is that you foul him before he scores and that he misses his free throws." Ah yes, the charity stripe. Like his long-ago Los Angeles predecessor, Wilt Chamberlain, Shaq is a terrible free throw shooter, which has kept him from averaging 30 points a game and being considered the league's best player. Hey, nobody's perfect.

Stat Attack   Career Highlights

Born:	March 6, 1972, Newark, NJ	**1992** Selected by the Orlando Magic with the first pick in the NBA Draft after a three-year career at Lousiana State
Ht/Wt:	7—1, 315 pounds	
School:	Louisiana State University	**1992** Became the first player in NBA history to be named Player of the Week in his first week in the league
Pro Career:	Orlando Magic (1992–96), Los Angeles Lakers (1996–)	**1993** Named NBA Rookie of the Year
		1995 Led the NBA in scoring while leading the Magic to first NBA Finals appearance in franchise history
Career Avgs:	27.1 ppg, 12.2 rpg, 2.5 apg	
		1997 Honored as one of the 50 Greatest Players in NBA History
		1999 Led the NBA in field goal percentage for the second season in a row

DAVID ROBINSON
San Antonio Spurs

$14,800,000 | 4

One of the game's most athletic and versatile big men — to say nothing of his squeaky-clean off-court image — David Robinson has perhaps shown his greatest value in the past two seasons as he's adopted a complementary role to teammate Tim Duncan. The somewhat passive Robinson who allowed Duncan to become the main man on the '99 Spurs team that led the Western Conference in wins may be a far cry from the take-charge DR who won the MVP award in 1995, but this one is no less valuable. Because even though his once-lethal scoring numbers have dropped with Duncan on board, the former ensign can still torpedo opponents in a number of ways.

The quick, lithe body Robinson unleashed on colleges back in the '80s as a star for the disrespected Academy remains perfect for defending against all opponents, and his textbook rebounding skills and leadership are invaluable. "David doesn't need to be a 30-point scorer for us anymore, but he's still our anchor," says Spurs head man Gregg Popovich. "He's busy rebounding, blocking shots, just taking pride in leading our defense."

Just as the Navy can take pride in the player and man they produced.

Stat Attack

Born:	August 6, 1965, Key West, FL
Ht/Wt:	7—1, 250 pounds
School:	Naval Academy
Pro Career:	San Antonio Spurs (1989–)
Career Avgs:	24.4 ppg, 11.5 rpg, 3.0 apg

Career Highlights

1987	Consensus choice for National College Player of the Year
1987	Selected with the first pick in the NBA Draft
1990	Named NBA Rookie of the Year, scoring 24.3 ppg despite a two-year absence from competitive basketball due to his military commitments
1994	Scored 71 points in the last game of the regular season to clinch the NBA scoring title
1995	Named NBA MVP
1996	Played on his third U.S. Olympic team ('88 and '92 were others)
1997	Honored as one of the NBA's 50 Greatest Players

SHAWN KEMP
Cleveland Cavaliers

$14,280,000 | 5

As befits an athletic player who never played a game in college, there have been two constants in Shawn Kemp's NBA career — plays that made you shake your head in awe or disgust, and an uncanny ability to improve every year. Known as "the Reign Man" when he would let loose with violent dunks as an exciting if undisciplined member of the Sonics, the Kemp of today's Cleveland Cavaliers is still entertaining but infinitely more polished. His high-flying slams have been replaced by an efficient jump shot; the lean leaper replaced by a big bruiser. And through it all, Kemp has gotten better. In '99, a year which saw most big scorers struggle to fill it up, Kemp dropped a career-high 20.5 points a night.

He's even become a leader for his youthful Cleveland teammates. "Off the court, we know we can talk to him about anything," says young teammate Brevin Knight. "And on the court, he's the key to our team getting open looks. When we give him the ball, the other team has to double-team him or else he'll score at will. When they do double, he's great at passing it out to us." When it rains, it pours.

Stat Attack

Born:	November 26, 1969, Elkhart, IN
Ht/Wt:	6—10, 280 pounds
School:	Concord High School
Pro Career:	Seattle SuperSonics (1989–97), Cleveland Cavaliers (1997–)
Career Avgs:	16.7 ppg, 9.5 rpg, 1.9 apg

Career Highlights

1991	Finished second in the NBA Slam-Dunk Contest
1994	Won a gold medal at the World Basketball Championships as a member of "Dream Team II"
1996	Led the Sonics with 23.3 ppg and 10 rpg in Seattle's NBA Finals appearance against Chicago
1997	Scored the 10,000th point of his career in his final season as a Sonic
1998	Started his fifth straight All-Star game, this time as the first such honoree in Cleveland history

SCOTTIE PIPPEN

Houston Rockets

$14,000,000   6=

There has perhaps been no NBA player who generates as much debate as Scottie Pippen. Everyone acknowledges the man's physical gifts and unbelievable instincts for the game. But is he a true, stand-alone superstar, or just the greatest complementary player ever? Even after more than a decade in the game, the jury may still be out.

Pip came out of tiny Central Arkansas and played his first season like a deer in headlights — homeboy was scared. But with the help of Michael Jordan, Scottie started to crawl out of his shell and show off a diverse game that all in the league envied. When MJ retired for a year and a half, Pippen showed he could score, but didn't win the same way. Similarly in '99, when Pip moved on to Houston as a free agent for the big bucks he'd deserved for so long, he played all right; but the W's didn't come as easy as when Mike was with him. "Scottie's a complete player," Houston center Hakeem Olajuwon says. "He's active on defense, skilled on offense, and he has the same goal as the rest of us — to bring another championship to Houston."

Do that, Scottie, and all questions will have been answered.

Stat Attack   Career Highlights

Born:	September 25, 1965, Hamburg, AK
Ht/Wt:	6—7, 228
School:	Central Arkansas
Pro Career:	Chicago Bulls (1987–1998), Houston Rockets (1999–)
Career Avgs:	17.8 ppg, 6.8 rpg, 5.4 apg

1987 Selected with the fifth overall pick in the NBA Draft

1992 Won an Olympic gold medal

1993 Won third straight title with the Bulls

1994 With MJ in retirement, Pippen stole the show at the All-Star Game, winning MVP honors

1997 Honored as one of the 50 Greatest Players in NBA History

1997 Set a record with seven made three-pointers in Game Three of the Finals

1997 Named to the NBA All-Defensive first team for the sixth straight season

1998 Won third straight Title (again) with the Bulls

HORACE GRANT

Orlando Magic

$14,000,000   6=

While never a true superstar, Ho Grant (not to be confused with his twin bro, Harvey) has forever served his employers well as a prototypical NBA power forward. After a solid college career at Clemson, Grant was drafted into the perfect situation for any young player — along with Scottie Pippen — onto a team that featured Michael Jordan. An aggressive and intelligent defender, Grant was a perfect complementary piece for Chicago as it won three straight titles in the early '90s.

Having developed his game and shown his worth as a Bull, Grant tested the free-agent market after the '94 season, and landed in Orlando, where the Magic paid him handsomely to protect Shaquille O'Neal. Shaq has obviously moved on since then, but the begoggled Grant remains a vital cog in Orlando's engine, capable of locking up opposing big men on defense and consistently hitting 18-footers on offense. For all of this, the Magic Kingdom is lucky to have him. "Horace is a professional player," says teammate Darrell Armstrong. "Any team would be lucky to have a guy like that, both for his defense and the way he hurts other teams with his jumper."

Stat Attack

Born:	July 4, 1965, Augusta, GA
Ht/Wt:	6—10, 245
School:	Clemson University
Pro Career:	Chicago Bulls (1987–94), Orlando Magic (1994–)
Career Avgs:	12.4 ppg, 8.7 rpg, 2.4 apg

Career Highlights

1987	Named ACC Player of the Year, the first Clemson player to be so named
1993	Won his third straight NBA Title, with the Chicago Bulls
1994	Named to his first and only All-Star game in his final season as a Bull
1994	Signed to the Orlando Magic to a huge free-agent contract, and promptly led the Magic to the '95 Finals
1997	Led the Magic in field goal percentage (52%), shooting over 50% for the 10th straight season

ALONZO MOURNING

Miami Heat

$12,000,000   8=

Alonzo Mourning is, quite simply, the NBA's most intimidating player. Possessing brute strength and the intensity of a professional hit-man, Zo has spent his entire career striking fear into opposing centers, making up for his lack of height with a will to win. For much of Mourning's career the above description was also a curse, because he let his emotions get the best of him, as he'd pick up technicals and devastating (to his team) ejections.

In '99, however, a smarter Mourning was on display. Oh, he still wanted to win, but he was no longer hurting his team with his determination. Instead, the new Mourning showed off an expanded offensive arsenal and a defensive tenacity unmatched by anyone in the league. For Mourning's efforts, the former Hoya picked up the '99 Defensive Player of the Year trophy and received consideration for league MVP. In the mind of Heat coach Pat Riley, however, Zo really was the MVP.

"Zo does everything we ask of him," Riley says. "He stops guys in the lane, he's gotten better at scoring, and of course, he's our emotional leader."

All that, and Mourning can still scare the shorts off of his opponents.

Stat Attack   Career Highlights

Born:	February 8, 1970, Chesapeake, VA	**1992**	In his senior season at Georgetown, named Big East Player of the Year, Defensive Player of the Year and Big East Tournament MVP, the first player to win all those honors in the same year
Ht/Wt:	6—10, 261		
School:	Georgetown University		
Pro Career:	Charlotte Hornets (1992–95), Miami Heat (1995–)	**1993**	Unanimously chosen to the NBA All-Rookie first team
		1996	Scored a career-high 50 points against Washington
Career Avgs:	21.0 ppg, 10.2 rpg, 1.5 apg	**1998**	Led Heat in scoring, field goal percentage and blocked shots
		1999	Led the NBA in blocked shots (3.91 pg), which helped him take home the Defensive Player of the Year Award

JUWAN HOWARD
Washington Wizards

$12,000,000 | **8=**

A poster child for the economic chaos that started to take over the NBA a few years back, the steady-but-unspectacular Howard picked up his monster contract in the summer of '96 after a crazy bidding war broke out between the then-Washington Bullets and the Miami Heat. Howard stayed in DC, and fans throughout the capital rejoiced. His time in DC has not been all roses, however. The pairing of Howard with former Michigan "Fab Five" teammate Chris Webber ended without a single Playoff victory and, left alone this past season, Howard showed he is not a superstar yet.

As he did at Michigan, Howard can certainly do some damage, mostly on offense with a low-post game that is of the textbook-perfect variety. He has also earned the faith of his owner, Abe Pollin. "We're going to buld around Juwan Howard," Pollin said. "Chris Webber's gone so Juwan is now the main forward and he's going to be a superstar in this league."

Brilliant fundamentals and a believing owner can only get you so far, however. For Washington fans to feel truly like they got the best of the battle for Howard's services in that fateful summer, JH must do a little more.

Stat Attack

Born:	February 7, 1973, Chicago, IL
Ht/Wt:	6—9, 250 pounds
School:	University of Michigan
Pro Career:	Washington Wizards (Bullets) (1994–)
Career Avgs:	19.3 ppg, 7.9 rpg, 3.5 apg

Career Highlights

1993	Appeared in the NCAA Final Four for the second straight time as a member of the "Fab Five" at Michigan
1995	Named to the NBA All-Rookie second team
1996	Played in the All-Star game in San Antonio
1996	Named NBA Player of the Month in March, the first Bullet to be so honored since '83
1996	Signed a lucrative contract extension with the Bullets
1999	Grabbed his 2,500th career rebound

HAKEEM OLAJUWON
Houston Rockets

$11,600,000   10

An essentially permanent part of the Houston skyline, Hakeem "The Dream" Olajuwon has been delighting fans in the Lone Star State for almost two decades. First as a Houston Cougar, and since '84 as a Rocket, Olajuwon has made his mark with grace. The former soccer goaltender came to the U.S. a gifted athlete, and once he picked up the nuances of the NBA game, Olajuwon became an unstoppable force on offense. After three brilliant collegiate seasons that all ended in the Final Four, the apex of Olajuwon's professional career came in '94 and '95, when he led an otherwise pedestrian Rockets team to two straight NBA titles, forever cementing his position as one of the greatest players in the history of the game. "There has never been a big man like Dream," says Rockets' head man Rudy Tomjanovich. "His size and defense combined with his moves are unbelievable."

Just as remarkable is that the run may not even be over yet. Drafted the same year as Michael Jordan, Olajuwon has played straight through and can still be counted on to score when needed. If he, Pippen and Barkley come back strong next year, the Dream Houston fans have may be a recurring one.

Stat Attack

Born:	January 21, 1963, Lagos, Nigeria
Ht/Wt:	7—0, 255 pounds
School:	University of Houston
Pro Career:	Houston Rockets (1984–)
Career Avgs:	23.6 ppg, 11.8 rpg, 2.7 apg

Career Highlights

1984	Left college with an 88–16 record over three seasons
1984	Selected first in the NBA Draft (ahead of Michael Jordan and Charles Barkley)
1985	Named to the NBA All-Rookie first team
1986	Appeared in the NBA Finals for the first time as the Rockets lost to the Celtics
1990	Recorded the third quadruple double in NBA history, notching 18 points, 16 rebounds, 11 blocks and 10 assists in a game versus the Clippers
1997	Honored as one of the 50 Greatest Players in NBA History
1999	Moved over 3,500 career blocks, good for first all-time in NBA history

DIKEMBE MUTOMBO
Atlanta Hawks

$11,400,000 | 11

ikembe Mutombo may be the least accomplished of the triad of Georgetown centers to enter the league (behind Ewing and Mourning), but he has proven himself to be a tremendously valuable player. With Mutombo's offensive game a work in progress, he has made his mark at the defensive end.

Beginning at G-Town, where Mutombo was named Big East Defensive Player of the Year after his senior season, and continuing in Denver and Atlanta, Mutombo has used his long arms and exceptional reflexes well enough to be that rare player who can change a game just by playing defense. "Defensively, Dikembe Mutombo has no equal at the center position," says former teammate Christian Laettner. "When people mention defensive centers, they think of him, and then they mention everyone else."

One other thing Mutombo has going for him is the fact that the only thuggery he commits is on the court. Off the floor, Mutombo may be the league's finest gentleman, visiting Africa in the off-season and building a hospital. If Mount Mutombo can add enough offense to complement his D and his heart, then he may become the most prominent Hoya Destroya.

Stat Attack | Career Highlights

Born:	June 25, 1966, Kinshasha, Congo (formerly Zaire)
Ht/Wt:	7—2, 265 pounds
School:	Georgetown University
Pro Career:	Denver Nuggets (1991–96), Atlanta Hawks (1996–)
Career Avgs:	12.9 ppg, 12.5 rpg, 1.5 apg

1991 Drafted fourth overall in the NBA Draft by the Denver Nuggets

1992 Scored a career-high 39 points against Minnesota

1994 Set an NBA record with 31 blocked shots in a five-game series, leading the eighth-seeded Nuggets over the first-seeded Sonics (the first time an 8 seed ever beat a 1)

1996 As a free agent, signed a five-year contract with the Hawks

1998 Led the NBA in total blocked shots for the fifth consecutive season

ANTONIO McDYESS

Denver Nuggets

$11,250,000   12

With a name that's fun to say, a game that's thrilling to watch and potential oozing from his agile bones, Antonio McDyess is one of the sure-fire NBA stars of the next millennium. Such a proclamation may have seeemed absurd when McDyess was a nobody through his first year and a half at Alabama, but ever since he burst on the scene in the '95 NCAA Tournament, McDyess has been a player to watch.

Ever since that tournament, as a result of which he was picked second in the draft, McDyess has made fans drool and opponents cry with a game that screams Power! "Dice" can kill you with his jams and one-handed boards, and a player who is known for just such activities recognizes the Second Coming. "He's strong inside, all over," says fellow-devastator Shawn Kemp. "You can look at the guy and see raw talent. My man can play."

Not only can McDyess play but his play is improving, as he showed by dropping career-high averages of 21.2 points and 10.7 rebounds a night last season. Clearly the man is still learning the game, so just imagine what he'll be doing in 2002.

Stat Attack   Career Highlights

Born:	September 7, 1974, Quitman, MS
Ht/Wt:	6—9, 220 pounds
School:	University of Alabama
Pro Career:	Denver Nuggets (1995–97), Phoenix Suns (1997–98), Nuggets (1999–)
Career Avgs:	16.6 ppg, 8.0 rpg, 1.3 apg

1995	First attracted attention when he scored 39 points and grabbed 19 rebounds in an NCAA Tournament game versus Pennsylvania
1996	Selected to the NBA All-Rookie first team
1998	Playing with the Suns, made his first Playoff appearance and averaged 18 ppg and 13 rpg in the Playoffs
1999	Spurned a bigger financial offer from the Suns to return to the Nuggets as a free agent
1999	Scored a career-high 46 points in a victory over the Grizzlies

GARY PAYTON
Seattle SuperSonics

$10,510,000   13

Once known strictly for his loud-mouth antics, the loquacious Gary Payton has moved into the upper echelon of the NBA by buckling down on defense and working hard on his once-limited offense. Ever since his days at OSU, GP was known as a talkative defender with lightning-quick hands, but he struggled to play the point guard position with consistency.

The days of waiting for offense are now long gone. GP has developed a wicked handle, solid passing ability and even a lethal shot from outside. Payton is now respected as a scorer, which makes him an even better passer since defenders have so much to worry about.

GP can still yap with the best of them, but his verbal skills have been harnessed to such a degree that Payton was the undeniable team leader for the '96 Sonic team which took the Bulls to six games in the NBA Finals, and remains the heart of the Sonics today.

"Gary's the type of guy that if you're both sitting down, he wants to see who can get up the fastest," says teammate Vin Baker. "That's how competitive he is. He just hates to lose." And he usually doesn't.

Stat Attack   Career Highlights

Born:	July 23, 1968, Oakland, CA	1990	Selected second overall in the 1990 NBA Draft
Ht/Wt:	6—4, 180 pounds	1991	Named to the NBA All-Rookie second team
School:	Oregon State University	1996	Named NBA Defensive Player of the Year
Pro Career:	Seattle SuperSonics (1990–)	1996	Just after competing against the Chicago Bulls in the NBA Finals, won a gold medal with the US Olympic Team in Atlanta
Career Avgs:	21.7 ppg, 3.8 rpg, 6.8 apg	1998	Played in his fourth straight All-Star game, picking up a game-high 13 assists
		1998	Named to the All-NBA first team
		1999	Notched his 1,500th career steal

ROD STRICKLAND
Washington Wizards

$10,000,000   14=

The fact that Rod Strickland's off-court life has been so chaotic — featuring trades, suspensions, and debate about his merits — belies the fact that when on the court, Strickland is one of the game's most consistent performers.

Strickland is a mercurial floor general, controlling the ball as if it's on a string, whipping no-look passes or sneaking into the lane for a crafty finger roll. And he does it all with a peaceful calm. Ever since the New York native debuted with the Knicks, teams have been wowed by his point play, but off-court incidents have led to trades across the NBA map.

No less an observer than Maurice Cheeks, perhaps the calmest, most mature point guard in NBA history, sees the effectiveness of Strickland. "Rod kind of goes at his own pace and runs the team in his own, graceful way. He breaks the defense down, penetrates and kicks the ball to other scorers. The mark of any true player is that someone doesn't want to play against him. I'm sure guys around the league say that when they have to play Rod."

Strickland — somehow never named to an All-Star team — is the eqivalent of Public Enemy in the late '80s: critically acclaimed, publically reviled.

Stat Attack   Career Highlights

Born:	July 11, 1966, Bronx, NY	
Ht/Wt:	6—3, 185 pounds	
School:	DePaul	
Pro Career:	New York Knicks (1988–90), San Antonio Spurs (1990–92), Portland TrailBlazers (1992–96), Washington Wizards/Bullets (1996–)	
Career Avgs:	15.0 ppg, 4.1 rpg, 8.0 apg	

1988	Selected in the first round of the NBA Draft by the team of his childhood, the New York Knicks
1989	Named to the NBA All-Rookie second team
1992	Led the Spurs in assists for the second straight season
1996	Led the Blazers in assists for the fourth straight season
1997	Scored his 10,000th career point
1998	Led the NBA in assists with a career-high average of 10.5 per game
1998	Named to the All-NBA second team

CHARLES OAKLEY

Toronto Raptors

$10,000,000 **14=**

A gritty and gutsy power forward, Charles Oakley is one of the NBA's hardest-working players, and he's still going strong even after 14 pro seasons. While always sporting a reliable 18-foot jumper, textbook rebounding skills and the ability to throw an around-the-back pass, the "Oak Tree" has perhaps been most valuable as a bodyguard to some of the league's most talented players.

During Oakley's first three seasons, he endeared himself to teammate Michael Jordan by always getting MJ's back if an opponent committed a hard foul. The tears of sadness that MJ cried when Oak got traded to New York were similar to the tears of joy of Knicks center Patrick Ewing. Throughout Oakley's 10 years in New York he did the dirty work inside while Ewing was able to set up outside the lane and perfect his jump shot. This past season saw Oakley take his blue-collar brand of ball north of the border, where he lent his physical services and emotional leadership to a young Raptors team that desperately needed it. "Charles Oakley was so good for us because he played such a physical, intimidating game," says Knicks' coach Jeff Van Gundy. "And yet he never got in foul trouble." That's Oak — solid and smart.

Stat Attack

Born:	Dec. 18, 1963
Ht/Wt:	6—9, 245 pounds
School:	Virginia Union
Pro Career:	Chicago Bulls (1985–88), New York Knicks (1988–98), Toronto Raptors (1999–)
Career Avgs:	10.6 ppg, 10.3 rpg, 2.5 apg

Career Highlights

1985	Drafted out of tiny Virginia Union by the Chicago Bulls
1986	Named to the NBA All-Rookie first team
1988	Led the NBA in total rebounds for the second straight season
1994	Played in his first and only All-Star game in Minneapolis
1998	Picked up the 10,000th point and rebound of his career by March of his 13th season
1998	Named to the NBA All-Defensive Second Team

RIK SMITS

Indiana Pacers

$10,000,000 **14=**

R ik Smits may go by the catchy nickname of "The Dunking Dutchman," but he has not lasted more than 10 years as a standout NBA center because of his dunking ability. Instead, the 7—4 big man has thrived with a silky-soft 15-footer that confounds his opposition.

Seen as a novelty — albeit one with some major potential — when he came out of unknown Marist University in '88, Smits has been known to frustrate teammates and coaches with his lack of rebounding or passing skills — but kick him a pass for a baseline shot and you might as well change the scoreboard; Smits' shot is going in. "You can be smothering him, thinking you have him covered..." says coach Tree Rollins, "but he'll just step back and use his size to shoot over you."

Besides his shot, Smits has been an effective tool for the Pacers on the inside, using his long arms frame to disturb any opponent who dares venture into the lane. Knowing Smits is sitting as a last line of defense has enabled the Pacers to gamble a bit more, and big Rik has played an undeniable role in the Pacers' maturation from Central Division laughing-stock to NBA power.

Stat Attack

Born:	August 23, 1966, Eindhoven, Holland
Ht/Wt:	7—4, 265 pounds
School:	Marist University
Pro Career:	Indiana Pacers (1988–)
Career Avgs:	15.0 ppg, 6.2 rpg, 1.4 apg

Career Highlights

1988	Scored a Marist record of 45 points in his final collegiate game
1988	Chosen with the second pick in the NBA Draft by the Pacers
1989	Named to the NBA All-Rookie first team
1995	Scored a career-high 44 points against the Los Angeles Clippers
1998	Elected to his first and only All-Star game in New York's Madison Square Garden

VLADE DIVAC
Sacramento Kings

$10,000,000 | **14=**

Loved throughout the NBA for his good humor and point guard-like passing ability, Divac spent 1999 reminding observers that he's also one hell of a player. Despite suffering through sleepness nights as he worried about family members in Europe, Divac averaged 16 points, 10 rebounds and five assists as the Kings came close to upsetting the Jazz in the Playoffs.

The assists Divac picked up throughout the Playoffs were no surprise since Vlade has always been an unselfish wizard with the ball, but the overall skills haven't always been so obvious. When Divac was with the Lakers, he gained notoriety for frustrating teammate Magic Johnson with his untapped potential. Today, even Magic and his Laker cohorts would have to admit that Divac is a force to be reckoned with. "I can still remember the day I picked Vlade up at the airport in Los Angeles," recalls Lakers' president Jerry West. "He got off the plane and looked like ... some damned vagabond. He was so young and didn't have much. And now look at him. I'm very happy things worked out for him in Sacramento because he's an absolutely delightful person." A delightful player too.

Stat Attack

Born:	February 3, 1968, Prijepolje, Yugoslavia
Ht/Wt:	7–1, 260 pounds
School:	N/A
Pro Career:	Los Angeles Lakers (1989–96), Charlotte Hornets (1996–98), Sacramento Kings (1998–)
Career Avgs:	12.5 ppg, 8.8 rpg, 2.9 apg

Career Highlights

1991	Named to the NBA All-Rookie first team
1991	Played in the NBA Finals as the Lakers lost to the Bulls
1996	Traded from the Lakers to the Hornets for Kobe Bryant
1996	Left the Lakers ranked third on the team's all-time blocked shots list
1996	Earned a silver medal at the Olympics with the Yugoslavian Olympic team
1999	Signed as a free agent with the Kings and then led Sacramento to a near-upset of the Utah Jazz in the first round of the Playoffs

CHRIS WEBBER

Sacramento Kings

$10,000,000   14=

Still just a young man of 26 years, Chris Webber has nonethess been through a career with more ups and downs than your craziest roller coaster. At Michigan he was the energetic leader of the "Fab Five" group of recruits, but then played a key role in the Wolverines' consecutive title losses. As a rookie with Golden State, Webber wowed the league with his skills, but warred so much with his autocratic coach Don Nelson that he was dealt to Washington. While he was in Washington Webber melded his offensive abilities — which allow him to beat his defender with power or finesse, brains or brawn — with a disturbing knack for getting hurt or running foul of the law.

Like Golden State, the Washington franchise tired of C-Webb's act, so much so that he was shipped West, to a Sacramento team for which many predicted he'd cause problems. Instead, says teammate Corliss Williamson, "He's real laid-back, a cool brother. Both on and off the court, he really helped us this year." Webber is, even for much of the media, as pleasant to talk to as anyone in the league, and even more fun to watch play. Seems like the roller coaster is finally on a permanent upswing.

Stat Attack

Born:	March 1, 1973, Detroit, MI
Ht/Wt:	6—10, 245 pounds
School:	University of Michigan
Pro Career:	Golden State Warriors (1993–94), Washington Bullets/Wizards (1994–98), Sacramento Kings (1999–)
Career Avgs:	20.0 ppg, 10.0 rpg, 4.2 apg

Career Highlights

1993	Appeared in his second straight NCAA Championship game with the Michigan Wolverines
1993	Drafted first overall by the Orlando Magic, then trade instantly to the Golden State Warriors, with whom he won the NBA's Rookie of the Year Award
1997	Chosen to his first All-Star game
1997	Led the Bullets in points, rebounds and blocked shots
1998	Averaged a career-high 21.9 ppg in his final season in Washington
1999	Led the NBA in rebounding (13.0 rpg) in his first season as a King

TOM GUGLIOTTA
Phoenix Suns

$9,750,000   19

With a little more time adjusting to the Phoenix Suns, Tom Gugliotta may finally emerge as a true star in the NBA. "Googs" grew from college nobody to first-round draft pick, and as a pro he's in the process of growing from complementary piece to "go-to" player.

While Gugliotta was, for the most part, slept on during his tours of duty with the Bullets and Warriors, he started to blossom as a Timberwolf during his years in Minnesota, showing off an effective jumper and rugged rebounding skills. Problem for TG was that the T'Wolves had two other rising stars in Kevin Garnett and Stephon Marbury. To escape the malaise of being a third wheel, Gugliotta took advantage of his free-agent status before the '99 season and moved to the desert, choosing to continue his development as a Phoenix Sun. With Phoenix, Googs can sit back, wait for point guard Jason Kidd to deliver him the ball, and then work his magic. "Googs is the perfect guy to play with since he can beat you so many ways," says Kidd.

Gugliotta's statistics actually went down in '99 but, again, the man had a lot to adjust to. Come next year, no one's going to want to guard him.

Stat Attack   Career Highlights

Born:	December 19, 1969, Huntington Station, NY	
Ht/Wt:	6—10, 240 pounds	
School:	NC State	
Pro Career:	Washington Bullets (1992–94), Golden State Warriors (1995), Minnesota Timberwolves (1995–98), Phoenix Suns (1999–)	
Career Avgs:	16.7 ppg, 8.8 rpg, 3.6 apg	

1992 Selected to the All-ACC first team, then chosen by the Bullets with the eighth pick in the draft

1992 Scored a career-high 39 points just one month into his NBA career

1993 Named to the NBA All-Rookie first team

1997 Made his All-Star debut

1999 Signed a long-term contract with the Phoenix Suns, then scored a game-high 24 points and grabbed a game-high 17 rebounds in the first game of the year

REGGIE MILLER
Indiana Pacers

$9,000,000 | 20

Yes, Reggie Miller is a one-dimensional player. Yes, he whines a lot. And yes, Knick fans, he's been an obnoxious opponent over the years. But MAN, has Mr. Miller had a career.

The man who possesses the NBA's most unorthodox shot has spent 12 seasons tormenting opponents with his ability seemingly never to miss. Truth be told, while Miller has always been a brilliant free throw shooter, he's only shot over 50% from the floor in four of his 12 seasons; but when a game is on the line, Reggie is the money man. He can barely dunk, and teammates are still waiting for the first time they see him beat a guy off the dribble, but when a screen is set for Miller and he catches that pass, look out. Furthermore, Miller will make that shot no matter where he is. The most prolific three-point shooter in NBA history, Miller can hurt you from 27 feet out as easily as 15. No less an authority than the Greatest Ever has weighed in on Miller's behalf. "Reggie steps up the way all great players do," said Michael Jordan during the '98 Playoffs. "When we forgot about him, he made shots."

Forget about Reggie Miller? Once a bad move, always a bad move.

Stat Attack | Career Highlights

Born:	August 24, 1965, Riverside, CA	1987	Drafted 11th overall by the Indiana Pacers
Ht/Wt:	6—7, 185 pounds	1992	Scored a career-high 57 points in a game versus the Charlotte Hornets
School:	UCLA		
Pro Career:	Indiana Pacers (1987–)	1994	The leading scorer and tri-captain of the USA Basketball Team that won the World Championships
Career Avgs:	19.7 ppg, 3.1 rpg, 3.1 apg	1995	Became the first Pacer ever chosen to start in the All-Star game
		1998	Chosen to the All-NBA Third Team for the third time, then led Pacers to within a game of the NBA Final before losing to the Bulls
		1999	Finished the season as the runaway leader in career three-pointers made (1,702) and attempted (4,225)

ANFERNEE HARDAWAY

Orlando Magic

$8,500,000   21

nfernee Hardaway, known to his multitude of fans simply as Penny, has spent the better part of his career on the cusp of stardom. In high school Penny was just beginning to receive acclaim when he got shot in front of his Memphis home. Hardaway came back enough to be an All-American collegian at the University of Memphis, and seemingly entered the NBA on a one-way track to immortality. However, after leading the Magic to the '95 NBA Finals and averaging a career-high 21.7 ppg in '96, he started getting hurt.

Injuries have hampered his game ever since and, due to difficulties in diagnosing exactly what's been wrong with him, Hardaway's motivation has been questioned. By the time next season comes around, don't be surprised if Penny Hardaway is with a team other than the Magic. Not that any team wouldn't love to have a guy who's 6—7 and equally adept at the point and two-guard positions. "Penny Hardaway is one of the NBA's most unique talents," says ex-Magic coach Richie Adubato. Adubato should know; in the '97 Playoffs versus Miami, he watched from the sideline as Penny took the Magic on his back and nearly upset the favored Heat.

Stat Attack   Career Highlights

Born:	July 18, 1971, Memphis, TN	1993	Selected third in the NBA Draft by the Warriors, then traded to the Magic
Ht/Wt:	6—7, 215 pounds	1994	Named MVP of the inaugural NBA Rookie All-Star game
School:	University of Memphis	1995	Named NBA Player of the Month for November
Pro Career:	Orlando Magic (1993–)	1996	Finished season as the only player in NBA to average more than 20 points and five assists while shooting better than 50% from the floor
Career Avgs:	19.0 ppg, 4.7 rpg, 6.3 apg	1996	Named to the All-NBA first team for the second season in a row
		1996	A member of the gold medal-winning US team at the Olympics
		1998	Made his fourth consecutive All-Star start

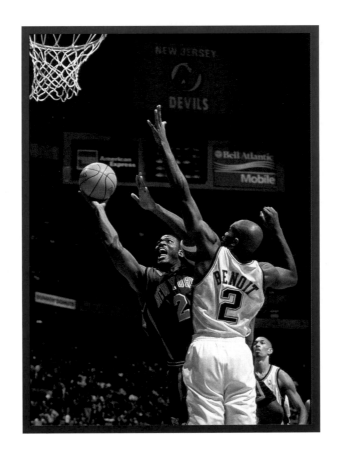

LARRY JOHNSON
New York Knicks

$8,460,000 | 22

arry Johnson is by no means the player he once was. But this is not an entirely bad thing. The LJ that skyed over opponents for power jams and one-handed glass work was sure fun to watch, but what did the Hornets ever do? Since his Charlotte days ended with a '96 trade to the Knicks, Johnson has been slowed and grounded by a deteriorating back; but rather than just giving up LJ has reinvented himself, proving to be one of the Knicks' most valuable players.

The new LJ beats you with hard work, fundamentally sound post play and demonstrative emotion. It's a package that Knicks head coach Jeff Van Gundy finds irresistible. "I'll tell you this; if there was a Larry Johnson Fan Club, I'd be the President."

That says a lot about Johnson, who has gone from the most popular player among young fans — LJ appeared in a Converse ad as "Grandmama" as a rookie, and was also featured on the first-ever cover of *SLAM* magazine, which is very popular among the NBA's teenage fans — to being revered by an old-fashioned coach like Van Gundy.

Stat Attack

Born:	March 14, 1969, Tyler, TX
Ht/Wt:	6—7, 235 pounds
School:	UNLV
Pro Career:	Charlotte Hornets (1991–96), New York Knicks (1996–)
Career Avgs:	17.6 ppg, 8.0 rpg, 3.5 apg

Career Highlights

1990	Won a College National Championship as UNLV beat Duke in the NCAA Title Game
1991	Consensus College Player of the Year after his senior year at UNLV
1991	Drafted first overall by the Charlotte Hornets
1992	Named NBA Rookie of the Year
1993	Named to the All-NBA second team after averaging a career-best 22 ppg
1995	Played in his second NBA All-Star game
1998	Scored a Knicks' career-high 35 points in a win over arch-rivals Miami

MICHAEL FINLEY

Dallas Mavericks

$8,000,000   23=

Despite playing in the relative anonymity of a Dallas franchise that hasn't been good in eons, unheralded small forward Mike Finley is slowly becoming a hell of a player. Despite a rock-solid four-year career at Wisconsin that saw him terrorize opponents throughout the staid Big 10 Conference, Finley wasn't even selected in the draft until the Phoenix Suns tabbed him at number 21. Nonetheless, Finley overlooked the slight and came into the NBA like a vet, scoring 15 a game in his first two years, even with a mid-season trade to Dallas in year two.

While Finley's athletic prowess is undeniable — the man could probably throw down his patented tomahawk jam on three defenders at the same time — Fin-Dog has earned even better reviews for all the intangibles he brings to the game. "People criticize today's young players for their work ethic, but Michael is above all that," says teammate AC Green. "He has the persona, desire and habits of a player who came into the league 10 years ago."

Once he does reach that 10-year status, some fans may even learn who Finley is. They'll be happy when they do.

Stat Attack

Born:	March 6, 1973, Melrose Park, IL
Ht/Wt:	6—7, 215 pounds
School:	University of Wisconsin
Pro Career:	Phoenix Suns (1995–97), Dallas Mavericks (1997–)
Career Avgs:	17.7 ppg, 4.9 rpg, 3.8 apg

Career Highlights

1996	Runner-up in the NBA Slam-Dunk Contest
1996	Named to the NBA All-Rookie team
1998	Scored a career-high 39 points against the Cavaliers
1998	Led the NBA in minutes with 41.4 per game
1999	Ended the season with a streak of 297 straight games played, one of the best in the league

ALLAN HOUSTON

New York Knicks

$8,000,000 **23=**

T he quintessential moments of Allan Houston's career would probably make you nod off with boredom. The guy isn't going to dunk in a defender's face, he's not going to grab his crotch and scowl at the camera, and he's definitely not going to yell. But what he does do is kill you softly, using a beautiful jump shot and peaceful demeanor to lead his volatile team with calm. Houston's picture-perfect jumper and coach-friendly attitude are likely due to the fact that his father was a coach. First as an assistant at Louisville, and then as head man at Tennessee (where Allen played for him), Wade Houston helped instill in Allan all the values that make him such a great guy to have on your team.

"Allan is a guy who I always wanted to see be a little more aggressive," says former Piston coach Doug Collins. "But he's still an extremely valuable player. His shot demands attention from the defense."

And about that stuff about him putting you to sleep; you may have noticed his series-winning shot against the Heat that led to a full-court dash for the camera. That was a special occasion.

Stat Attack | Career Highlights

Born:	April 20, 1971, Louisville, KY	1993	Drafted in the first round by the Detroit Pistons
Ht/Wt:	6—6, 200 pounds	1995	Matched an NBA single-game record by hitting seven three-pointers in the first half of a game versus the Bulls
School:	University of Tennessee		
Pro Career:	Detroit Pistons (1993–96), New York Knicks (1996–)	1996	Made his Knicks' debut a successful one by scoring a team-high 28 points versus the Raptors
		1998	Scored his 6,000th career point
Career Avgs:	15.3 ppg, 2.8 rpg, 2.3 apg	1999	Selected for the 1999 USA basketball team

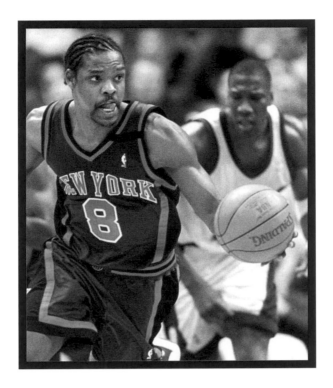

LATRELL SPREWELL

New York Knicks

$8,000,000 23=

New York's latest superstar, Latrell Sprewell, used the 1999 season to help repair an image that had taken a beating after he attacked Golden State Warriors' coach PJ Carlesimo in December of 1997. After being suspended for the remainder of the season, Spree was traded to the Knicks before the 1999 season and energized New York with his athletic and enthusiastic play.

The ugly incident with Carlesimo had Sprewell initially labeled as a poster boy for the troubles of the new NBA, but his play as the Knicks' sixth man in the '99 Playoffs had everyone singing a new tune. "Spree brings so much energy onto the court," says teammate Allan Houston. "He comes in so hyped up and instantly changes the game."

While the Sprewell that did damage out West often played all 48 minutes and shot 'til his arm fell off for a miserable Golden State franchise, he's been a true warrior off the bench for New York, delivering defense, hustle and scoring punch. Spree also achieved notoriety in the Spring of '99 when he filmed a commercial for the shoe company And 1 in which he called himself "the embodiment of the American Dream." To many, he is just that.

Stat Attack

Born:	September 8, 1970, Milwaukee, WI
Ht/Wt:	6—5, 190 pounds
School:	Alabama
Pro Career:	Golden State Warriors (1992–1998), New York Knicks (1999–)
Career Avgs:	19.8 ppg, 4.3 rpg, 4.5 apg

Career Highlights

1992	Named to the SouthEastern Conference's All-League First Team after his senior season at Alabama
1993	Named to the NBA All-Rookie Second Team
1994	Named to the All-NBA First Team and the All-Defensive Second Team after playing a league-high 43.1 minutes per game
1997	Led the Western Conference with 19 points in the All-Star Game in his third All-Star appearance
1997	Led the Warriors in scoring with a career-high 24.2 points per game, good for fifth in the NBA
1999	Knicks' Playoff MVP

KENNY ANDERSON

Boston Celtics

$7,000,000   26=

W hile "Kenny the Kid" may not be so young any more, it's not hard to recall a time when Kenny Anderson was the most entertaining player in the country. A New York City high school phenomenon since 9th Grade, when the time came for college, Anderson took his original point guard skills to Georgia Tech, where he wowed the nation with a handle the likes of which had never been seen.

The NYC native was later hailed as the savior of the Nets' franchise when New Jersey drafted him after his soph season at G-Tech, and he came through for a little while, but when super-coach Chuck Daly left the Nets, KA's game started to slip a bit. He recaptured the magic in Portland for a while, but after a year and a half there he was shipped to Boston.

Playing under Rick Pitino's run-and-gun style should suit Kenny just fine, but it may take a while. "Kenny's gonna be great in Boston," says fellow-NYC point man Rod Strickland. "They play an up-tempo game, and Kenny is one of the best in the league when he's in the open court."

Maybe even good enough to take you back a decade or so.

Stat Attack

Born:	October 9, 1970, Queens, NY
Ht/Wt:	6—1, 168 pounds
School:	Georgia Tech University
Pro Career:	New Jersey Nets (1991–96), Charlotte Hornets (1996), Portland Trail Blazers (1996–98), Boston Celtics (1998–)
Career Avgs:	15.1 ppg, 3.4 rpg, 7.3 apg

Career Highlights

1991	Drafted second overall by the New Jersey Nets
1994	Chosen to start in the All-Star Game
1994	Scored a career-high 45 points against the Pistons
1996	Traded from the Nets, leaving New Jersey as the franchise's all-time leader in assists (2,363)
1997	Led the 'Blazers in scoring (17.5 ppg), assists (7.1 apg) and steals (2 spg) while playing in all 82 games
1998	Scored a team-high 19 points in his first game as a Celtic

ELDEN CAMPBELL
Charlotte Hornets

$7,000,000 **26=**

A talented big man with a wide variety of skills, Elden Campbell has spent his career ably backing up guys like Vlade Divac and Shaquille O'Neal. As he enters his 10th season, however, look for Elden Campbell to finally become a star in his own right.

Because of Campbell's ability to score with ease, but also his propensity for mediocre defense, the Lakers viewed Campbell merely as backup quality from the day they drafted him. He never disappointed — even scoring 15 ppg in the '96–97 season — but he also never showed that he was ready to be a "go-to" guy. Enter the Hornets. Knowing that Glen Rice wanted out of Charlotte and that the Lakers were desperate for outside shooting, the Hornets eagerly took Campbell and Eddie Jones as compensation for their disgruntled shooter.

Many fans looked at Campbell as a mere throw-in in the deal, but Hornets coach Paul Silas had different ideas. "We're going to challenge Elden," he says. "With a little work we think he could be one of the best centers in the game."

Silas showed his faith in Campbell was for real, inserting EC into the starting lineup and running plays for him. It was a long time coming.

Stat Attack

Born:	July 23, 1968, Los Angeles, CA
Ht/Wt:	7—0, 255 pounds
School:	Clemson University
Pro Career:	Los Angeles Lakers (1990–99), Charlotte Hornets (1999–)
Career Avgs:	10.6 ppg, 6.0 rpg, 1.2 apg

Career Highlights

1990	Drafted in the first round by the Los Angeles Lakers
1991	Appeared in the NBA Finals as a rookie when the Lakers battled the Bulls
1997	Became just the seventh player in NBA History to improve his scoring average for his first seven years as a pro
1998	Blocked the 1,000th shot of his career, good for second in Lakers' franchise history
1999	Traded to the Hornets and promptly led them on a rush for the Playoffs

DERRICK COLEMAN
Charlotte Hornets

$7,000,000   26=

On one hand, Derrick Coleman possess all the tools that make a great basketball player. He's tall and wide, with amazing physical capabilities. He can run, jump, dribble, pass and shoot, both with range and touch. On the other, DC has yet to use all those skills to his full advantage, and what might have been a brilliant career has been plagued by injuries and off-court chaos.

In college, Coleman was a dominant force, even as a freshman, when he led Syracuse to the National Title Game. Coleman's peak as a professional came in '93 and '94 with the Nets, when he was a scoring, passing and shot-blocking monster, twice bringing the Nets within a game of Playoff upsets. "The key to Derrick Coleman is getting through to him," says Paul Silas, a former Net Assistant and the current head coach in Charlotte. "If you do that, you're going to be pleased with the results."

Considering Charlotte invested some big money in Coleman before last season, they obviously think he can fulfill that potential. As always, the key wil. be DC's attitude. If he stays in shape and plays hard, he can be one of the best.

Stat Attack

Born:	June 21, 1967, Mobile, AL
Ht/Wt:	6—10, 260 pounds
School:	Syracuse University
Pro Career:	New Jersey Nets (1990–95), Philadelphia 76ers (1995–98), Charlotte Hornets (1998–)
Career Avgs:	18.8 ppg, 10.3 rpg, 3.0 apg

Career Highlights

1990	Left Syracuse University after a four-year career as the school's all-time leading scorer and rebounder
1990	Drafted first overall by the Nets
1991	Named NBA Rookie of the Year
1994	Member of the US gold medal-winning team at the World Championships in Toronto
1994	Named to All-NBA Third Team for the second consecutive year
1999	Signed to a long-term free-agent contract by the Charlotte Hornets

GLENN ROBINSON
Milwaukee Bucks

$6,800,000   29

There were more than a few people disgusted when Glenn Robinson signed his first NBA contract. A high-scoring forward out of Purdue, Robinson was drafted first overall by the Bucks in the last year before rookie salary caps were imposed, and he promptly held out until just before the season's first game. When he finally did sign — for a whopping 10 years and $68 million — casual fans were enraged.

To say the least, no one's yelling anymore. Big Dog may not be the greatest player in the league, but how many players can be counted on to drop 20 points every night? Not many; but with an old-fashioned game that features solid post-up moves and a deadeye jumpshot, Robinson can. And there's a reason. "Glenn is not a flamboyant player, just very solid," says teammate Andrew Lang. "Every night you can count on his numbers because he's a hard worker that you know is going to come to play."

If there's a downside to Robinson's game, it's his mediocre rebounding and defense. But again, in the '90s NBA with points at a premium, Big Dog is an invaluable asset.

Stat Attack   Career Highlights

Born:	January 10, 1973, Gary, IN	1994	Won John Wooden Award as the nation's top collegiate player
Ht/Wt:	6—7, 230 pounds	1994	Drafted first overall by the Bucks
School:	Purdue University	1995	Named to the NBA All-Rookie Team
Pro Career:	Milwaukee Bucks (1994–)	1996	Scored a career-high 44 points versus the Bullets
Career Avgs:	21.1 ppg, 6.1 rpg, 2.9 apg	1998	Led his team and finished second in the league in minutes per game (41)

NICK ANDERSON

Orlando Magic

$6,700,000 | 30

Despite being a prototypical '90s two-guard who possesses strength, size and a wondrous outside shot, Nick Anderson existed on the periphery of fans' minds until he did something wrong. It came in the 1995 NBA Finals, when Anderson and his precocious teammates had taken a big lead in Game One against the Houston Rockets. The lead eventually shrank, but Anderson had a chance to clinch a Magic victory by hitting any one of four consecutive free throws. He missed them all.

Crushed, Anderson disappeared for the rest of the Finals, and wasn't much of a factor throughout '96 and '97, reaching his nadir when he shot a woeful 40% from the free throw line in the '96–97 season. When the calendar turned to '98, however, Nick was reborn, suddenly hitting his jumpers again and adding a new low-post game as well. Finally, the one member of the Orlando franchise who's been around since its inception was getting love for his play. "Nick's rebirth has been absolutely amazing," says recently-retired Magic coach Chuck Daly. "He's playing tremendous basketball, and I think any coach in the league would love to have him."

Stat Attack

Born:	January 20, 1968, Chicago, IL
Ht/Wt:	6—6, 220 pounds
School:	Illinois
Pro Career:	Orlando Magic (1989–)
Career Avgs:	15.4 ppg, 5.3 rpg, 2.8 apg

Career Highlights

1989 The first ever pick of the Orlando Magic franchise, Anderson was chosen 11th overall in the Draft

1992 Led Magic in scoring with 20 ppg

1995 Appeared in the NBA Finals with the Magic

1997 Signed a six-year contract extension with the Magic

1998 Named NBA Player of the Week in February, signalling his rebirth as a premier player by averaging 31 ppg and 7 rpg for the week

GRANT HILL
Detroit Pistons

$6,500,000   31

If the powers-that-be within the NBA had their wish, Grant Hill would be the next Michael Jordan. The man is smooth, smart and fun to watch, so it's no wonder that big companies like Fila and Sprite have used Hill to sell their products. Things have not gone quite as smoothly for Hill on the court as off, but that's not his fault. What the gifted Hill, who can score, rebound and play the unique "point forward" position, needs to be the true next Jordan are some Scottie Pippen-like teammates.

In the '98–99 season, Hill's Pistons were knocked out in the first round of the Playoffs, continuing Hill's streak of never having won a Playoff series. Hill will be a free agent after the 2000 season, and if things don't improve in Detroit he may move on. The league is already abuzz about where he may end up, and you can be sure he'll pick up the maximum allowable salary no matter where he goes. Whoever gets Hill would be wise to listen to long-time teammate Joe Dumars. "This man's the truth. I feel privileged to play with him. In 15 years — you watch — I'll be telling my children: 'See that guy? I played with him.'"

Stat Attack

Born:	May 10, 1972, Dallas, TX
Ht/Wt:	6—8, 225 pounds
School:	Duke University
Pro Career:	Detroit Pistons (1994–)
Career Avgs:	20.7 ppg, 8.1 rpg, 6.5 apg

Career Highlights

1991	Won the first of two straight NCAA Titles for Duke University
1994	Drafted third overall by the Pistons
1995	Named NBA co-Rookie of the Year along with Jason Kidd
1996	Won an Olympic gold medal with the US's "Dream Team II"
1998	Led NBA in triple-doubles with four
1998	Named to the All-NBA Second Team
1999	Scored a career-high 46 points versus the Wizards

KARL MALONE

Utah Jazz

$6,100,000 | 32

I f you're creating a "Team of the Era," Karl Malone at power forward is a sure pick. Ever since his second season, Malone has been the prototypical scoring power forward. Between '88 and '92, Malone never averaged fewer than 28 points a game. Those are numbers that cannot be messed with.

Due to the humble, almost rural nature that Malone brought with him from his native Louisiana, for the longest time Malone felt comfortable playing for a wage well below his market value. Well, that'll change next year. Malone and the Jazz have announced a contract extension that will pay him somewhere in the neighborhood of $16 million a year for the next four years, an impressive figure for a guy who's going to be 36 when the contract starts. Even if his play starts to drop off, however, Malone deserves the big payday for all that he's meant to the Jazz and the entire NBA throughout his career.

"Night in and night out he is the best power forward in the NBA," says long-time NBA coach Bill Fitch. "There are some guys who have as much ability as him, but no one else has that consistency and competitive fire every single night."

Stat Attack | Career Highlights

Born:	July 24, 1963, Summerfield, LA	1985	Drafted in first round of NBA Draft by Utah Jazz
Ht/Wt:	6—9, 255 pounds	1989	Named MVP of the All-Star Game
School:	Louisiana Tech	1990	Scored a career-high 61 points against the Milwaukee Bucks
Pro Career:	Utah Jazz (1985–)	1992	A member of the original "Dream Team," which won Olympic gold
Career Avgs:	26.1 ppg, 10.7 rpg, 3.3 apg	1997	Honored as one of the 50 Greatest Players in NBA History
		1997	Won his first-ever NBA MVP award
		1998	Selected to his 11th All-Star Game
		1999	Scored his 28,000th career point — the fourth-highest total in history
		1999	Named NBA MVP for the second time

EDDIE JONES
Charlotte Hornets

$6,000,000   33=

Eddie Jones is easily one of the NBA's most exciting players. Possessing a long body that seemingly gets from one end of the court to the other in about three strides, Jones is best known for his graceful slam-dunks and his consummate jump shot.

After a solid career at Temple University, Jones seemed to fit in well with the run-and-gun Lakers, at least for a while. But once L.A. picked up Shaq and Kobe Bryant, the spotlight unfortunately started to leave EJ. Jones ended up getting dealt to the Hornets this past season, and instantly resumed his sweet offensive play.

Says former Temple teammate and current Knick Ric Brunson: "Eddie — man, that guy could score. College, NBA, it doesn't matter. You get him the ball and he'll score for you."

Even when you're not in the mood for basketball on a highwire, Jones can still be the man to watch. Unlike some scorers, Jones is more than willing to slap on the tight D as well. Consistently among the league leaders in steals, Jones combines his athletic body with lightning-quick hands to make life miserable for opposing two-guards — on offense and defense.

Stat Attack

Born:	October 20, 1971, Toledo, OH
Ht/Wt:	6—6, 200 lbs.
School:	Temple University
Pro Career:	Los Angeles Lakers (1994–99), Charlotte Hornets (1999–)
Career Avgs:	15.4 ppg, 3.8 rpg, 3.1 apg

Career Highlights

1994	Drafted in the first round by the Lakers
1995	Won the MVP Award at the Rookie All-Star Game held during All-Star Weekend
1997	Scored a career-high 35 points versus the Kings
1997	Named NBA Player of the Month for November
1998	Named to the NBA All-Defensive Second Team
1998	Led the Lakers with 143 three-pointers made

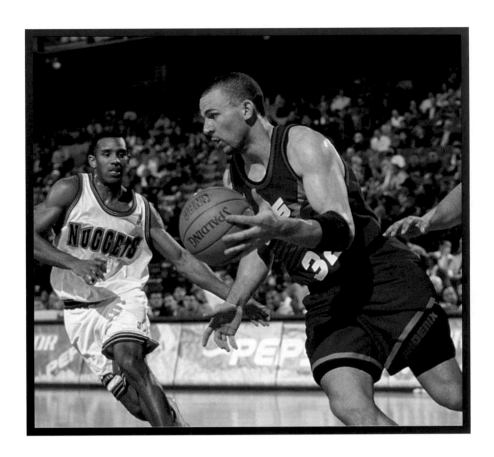

JASON KIDD
Phoenix Suns

$6,000,000 **33=**

J ason Kidd excels at a part of the game that receives scant attention — passing. The man may have an ugly jump shot and minimal jumping ability, but just watch him control things on a three-on-two fast break. What you're watching is a thing of beauty.

Kidd has been talked about in basketball circles since his high school days, when fans started whispering about some Magic Johnson clone that was doing work in the Bay Area. Calling Kidd "Magic-like" may be a bit of an exaggeration, but JK is indeed unparalleled as a passer in today's NBA.

"Playing with Jason is so simple," says teammate Tom Gugliotta. "Get to a spot you want to be in, and he'll get you the ball."

Kidd has spent the last few summers working on his jumper and, while it still looks ugly, he did shoot a career-high 44% from the field in '99. Add that to the passing and his tough on-the-ball defense and people are going to start talking about him in a whole new light. The new words that precede his name are going to sound a lot like "MVP candidate."

Stat Attack | Career Highlights

Born:	March 23, 1973, San Francisco, CA	1994	Selected second overall in the NBA Draft by the Dallas Mavericks
Ht/Wt:	6—4, 212 pounds	1995	Named NBA co-Rookie of the Year along with Grant Hill
School:	California		
Pro Career:	Dallas Mavericks (1994–97), Phoenix Suns (1997–)	1996	Passed for a career-high and Mavericks-record 25 assists in a game against the Jazz
		1998	Made his second career All-Star appearance
Career Avgs:	13.5 ppg, 6.0 rpg, 9.1 apg	1999	Led the NBA in assists
		1999	Named to the All-NBA Defensive First Team

ROBERT HORRY

Los Angeles Lakers

$6,000,000 **33=**

The best way to describe Lakers forward Robert Horry (don't pronounce the 'H') is "a poor man's Scottie Pippen." Everything that Pip can do — rebound, play defense on opposing point guards, shooting guards or forwards, knock down three-pointers — Horry can do, only maybe not as well.

The versatile Alabama product is also known as an extremely reliable player in crunch time. While Hakeem Olajuwon was obviously the centerpiece of the Rockets' back-to-back NBA Titles in '94 and '95, you can be sure that Houston wouldn't have won those rings without Horry's help. Throughout both Playoff runs, it was Horry that had the knack for the key steal or required three-pointer. As a result, Horry is considered a remarkably valuable player, even if his skills aren't all that amazing.

"Robert meant everything to our team," says Olajuwon. "I think he's one of the best players in the world."

Since '97 Horry's been doing it all for the Lakers, and if they ever put things together enough to make a title run, count on Horry to be right in the middle of it.

Stat Attack | Career Highlights

Born:	August 25, 1970, Hartford, MD	1993	Named to the NBA All-Rookie Second Team
Ht/Wt:	6—10, 235 pounds	1995	Scored a career-high 40 points versus the Milwaukee Bucks
School:	University of Alabama	1995	Won his second straight NBA Title with the Houston Rockets
Pro Career:	Houston Rockets (1992–96), Phoenix Suns (1996–97), Los Angeles Lakers (1997–)	1996	Set a Rockets franchise record with nine three-pointers in one game
		1997	Playing with the Lakers in the Playoffs, set an NBA Playoff record by hitting seven three-pointers without a miss
Career Avgs:	9.3 ppg, 5.4 rpg, 2.7 apg		

SHAWN BRADLEY
Dallas Mavericks

$5,940,000   36

I f blocked shots were the most important statistic in basket-ball, Shawn Bradley would be the NBA's most famous player. Instead, being that a successful basketball player needs to score every once in a while — not to mention stay out of foul trouble — Bradley's career has had more downs than ups.

Bradley was a phenomenon during his freshman season at BYU, blocking tons of shots and effectively changing the balance of power in the Western Athletic Conference. After that season, however, Bradley (a devout Mormon) went on a two-year missionary. Rather than coming back to work on the parts of his game that needed help, Bradley shocked the NBA by declaring for the Draft. The 76ers fell for his potential, tapping him with the second pick. Ultimately the 'Sixers gave up on Big Shawn, as they got sick of his penchant for foul trouble and a work ethic that is rumored to be lax.

Bradley's now with his third pro team, but the issues surrounding him remain the same. "When he plays with intensity, Shawn Bradley is one of the rare players who can single-handedly change the game," says Mavs coach Don Nelson. Problem is, "when" doesn't happen very often.

Stat Attack   Career Highlights

Born:	March 22, 1972, Landstuhl, West Germany	1991	Finished his first and only season at Brigham Young with 177 blocked shots, good for the NCAA Freshman record
Ht/Wt:	7—6, 263 pounds		
School:	Brigham Young University	1994	Named to the NBA All-Rookie Second Team
Pro Career:	Philadelphia 76ers (1993–96), New Jersey Nets (1996–97), Dallas Mavericks (1997–)	1995	Set 76ers franchise record with 274 blocks on the season
		1997	Tied career-high and set Mavericks franchise record for centers when he scored 32 points versus Clippers
Career Avgs:	11.0 ppg, 7.9 rpg, 0.9 apg	1998	Scored 22 points, grabbed 22 rebounds and had 13 blocks against Portland to become just the fifth player in NBA History to have a 20–20–10 triple-double

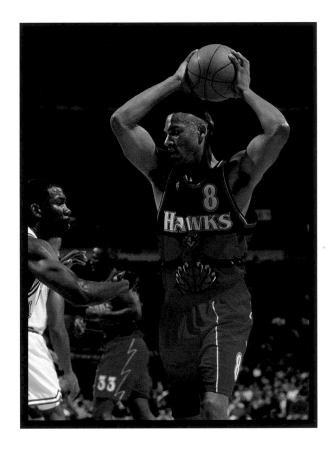

STEVE SMITH
Atlanta Hawks

$5,400,000   37=

Steve Smith has a lot of things going for him, and his unique, rugged scoring ability is only one of them. Just as important is an unselfishness that is seen in very few NBA players. This trait is seen first on the court, where the 6—8 Smith eschews hogging the ball the way he could, in order to be a true play-maker. Just like at Michigan State University, Smith has spent his NBA career making things happen for those around him. Even though he's got the size and skills of an off-guard, you're just as likely to see Smith make a sweet dish as take a three-pointer. If Smith played with dudes that could shoot a little better than his current team-mates, you'd wouldn't be surprised to see him average well over five assists a night while remaining a legitimate scoring threat.

"As far as I'm concerned, Steve Smith can shoot it whenever he wants. He's that good." So says Hawks' coach Lenny Wilkens.

As generous as Smith is on the court, he is even more so off the court. The highlight of Smith's altruism came in '97, when he gave a whopping $2.5 million to his alma mater to benefit student athletes.

Born:	March 31, 1969, Highland Park, MI
Ht/Wt:	6—8, 215 pounds
School:	Michigan State University
Pro Career:	Miami Heat (1991–1994), Atlanta Hawks (1994–)
Career Avgs:	17.4 ppg, 3.9 rpg, 4.1 apg

1991	Drafted in the first round by the Miami Heat
1994	Member of the gold medal-winning US basketball team at the World Championships
1997	Scored a career-high 41 points against the Utah Jazz
1998	Played in his first NBA All-Star Game
1998	Given the NBA's ultimate off-court honor when he won the J. Walter Kennedy Citizenship Award for the 1997–98 season

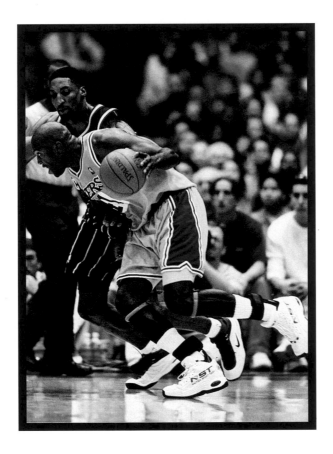

GLEN RICE

Los Angeles Lakers

$5,400,00 **37=**

When he was acquired in a trade this past season, Glen Rice was supposed to be the final piece in the puzzle for the enigmatic Los Angeles Lakers. The Lakers had reason for such optimism, because in an age of miserable outside shooting Glen Rice is cash from the outside. "G Money" is the guy you want to shoot an open (or even covered) 22-footer because odds are it'll go in. Of course, the Lakers of Shaq and Kobe Bryant proved unchangeable, even by a wizard like Rice. After having the entire Charlotte offense run through him for the past three seasons, Rice was the Lakers' third option. When the Lakers got bounced from the Playoffs in ugly fashion, people started to wonder: should Rice have gotten the ball more? The answer is, "of course." Just listen to what long-time Celtic Robert Parish says: "You want to know who else I put in Glen's category as a shooter? Larry Bird."

Being compared to Bird is no joke, and neither is Rice's pending free agency. Unless the Lakers make a commitment to utilize their marksman better, Rice may be with his fourth NBA squad next year. One thing's for sure:whoever it is will be lucky to have him.

Stat Attack

Born:	May 28, 1967, Jacksonville, AK
Ht/Wt:	6—8, 220 pounds
School:	University of Michigan
Pro Career:	Miami Heat (1989–95), Charlotte Hornets (1995–99), Los Angeles Lakers (1999–)
Career Avgs:	20.6 ppg, 4.7 rpg, 2.3 apg

Career Highlights

1989	Won a National Championship in his final season at the University of Michigan
1989	Drafted in the first round by the Miami Heat
1995	Scored a career-high, Miami Heat franchise-high and NBA season-high 56 points against the Magic
1997	Named MVP of the All-Star Game after scoring a record 20 points in the third quarter and scoring 26 for the game
1997	Finished the season with a career-best 26.7 ppg average, good for third in the league
1998	Named to the All-NBA Third Team

SEAN ELLIOTT
San Antonio Spurs

$5,330,000   39

A t least for a while, people forgot about Sean Elliott. They forgot about the collegian who was the nation's best player when he played for hometown Arizona. They forgot about the NBAer who scored with ease early in his pro career. The memory loss was prompted by a string of injuries that forced Elliott to miss more than half of his team's games in the '96–97 and '97–98 seasons.

By the time the '99 season finally got started, Elliott was almost a complete afterthought. On a team that has David Robinson and Tim Duncan, who had time to worry about a small wiry forward? Elliott didn't change that many minds during a '99 season that never saw him never score more than 22 points in a single game, but in the '99 Playoffs Elliott has once again been a man to watch. Elliott sparked the Spurs to key victories over the Portland TrailBlazers, including an improbable Game Two win that Elliott locked up with a last-second bomb that is already being called "The Shot" by San Antonio fans.

"Sean is just a great guy to play with," says former Arizona and current Spur teammate Steve Kerr. "He's one of the nicest guys in the league, and on the court you can count on him to score."

Stat Attack

Born:	February 2, 1968, Tucson, AZ
Ht/Wt:	6—8, 220 pounds
School:	University of Arizona
Pro Career:	San Antonio Spurs (1989–93), Detroit Pistons (1993–94), Spurs (1994–)
Career Avgs:	14.9 ppg, 4.5 rpg, 2.7 apg

Career Highlights

1989	Awarded the John Wooden Award as the nation's top collegiate player
1989	Drafted in the first round by the Spurs
1993	Appeared in his first-ever NBA All-Star Game
1997	Swiped his 500th career steal
1999	Played every game of the season for the first time since the 1991–92 season

RON HARPER

Chicago Bulls

$5,300,000 | 40

One of the first players to be labeled as the "Next Jordan," Ron Harper's career has had a number of distinct stages. He started as a legitimate threat to Jordan's throne, averaging 22.9 ppg in a rookie campaign that was filled with acrobatic lay-ups and high-flying jams. An injury in his second season with the Cavs ended the Jordan talk; but Harp remained a solid — if closer to the ground — player into the '89–90 season, at which point he'd been traded to the Clippers. In the middle of that fateful season, however, Harper suffered his second serious injury, a torn knee ligament that sidelined him for a year.

By the time Harper came back from injury number two, he was a shadow of his former self, at least physically. But the gritty veteran had learned the mental aspects of the game, and became one of those guys any team is happy to have. Phase three of Harp's career has included a five-year run with the Bulls that included three straight NBA Championships.

"Obviously Michael and Scottie were the stars of our team, but Ron Harper is the type of key complementary player you need to win titles," says former Bulls coach Phil Jackson.

Stat Attack

Born:	January 20, 1964, Dayton, OH
HtWt:	6—6, 216 pounds
School:	Miami of Ohio
Pro Career:	Cleveland Cavaliers (1986–90), Los Angeles Clippers (1990–94), Chicago Bulls (1994–)
Career Avgs:	14.8 ppg, 4.3 rpg, 4.0 apg

Career Highlights

1986	Named MVP of the Mid-American Conference for the second consecutive season
1986	Drafted eighth overall by the Cavaliers
1987	Named to the NBA All-Rookie First Team
1994	Averaged a team-high 20.1 ppg for the Clippers
1998	Won his third straight NBA Title with the Chicago Bulls

JOHN STARKS
Golden State Warriors

$5,100,000 | 41

Even at age 33, John Starks remains one of the NBA's most energetic players. A relative unknown when he came out of Oklahoma State, Starks got a brief job with the Warriors, but was cut after one season and returned to his native Oklahoma for a slightly different line of work — bagging groceries.

Starks maintained a dream of playing in the Big Leagues, though, and after a stint in the CBA he got picked up by the New York Knicks. At first, the country-living Starks seemed like a bad fit for the Big Apple, but within a year he had actually become a crowd favorite. The reasons for his ascension were an infectious enthusiasm and an ability to hit game-changing shots. There have always been players with more talent than Starks, but few have more heart. Jeff Van Gundy, Starks' coach when the latter was in NY, says this: "I love John as a player; love his competitive instincts, love how he approaches big games, the way he cares about the team."

Starks was a casualty of the Knicks' acquisition of Latrell Sprewell, getting shipped to G-State before the '99 season began. No matter, as he brought the same heart to the West Coast that he'd always shown in New York.

Stat Attack

Born:	August 10, 1965, Tulsa, OK
Ht/Wt:	6—5, 185 pounds
School:	Oklahoma State
Pro Career:	Golden State Warriors (1888–89), New York Knicks (1990–98), Warriors (1999–)
Career Avgs:	13.6 ppg, 2.6 rpg, 3.9 apg

Career Highlights

1991	Signed as a free agent by the Knicks
1993	Named to the NBA All-Defensive Second Team
1994	Played in the NBA All-Star Game
1994	Reached the NBA Finals as a member of the Knicks
1994	Honored by the City of Tulsa with an official "John Starks Day"
1999	Made his 1,000th career three-pointer

ANTONIO DAVIS

Indiana Pacers

$5,000,000   42=

Antonio Davis pretty much defines the term "late bloomer." AD was actually drafted by the Pacers in 1990, a second-round pick out of UTEP (where he played with Tim Hardaway), but rather than try the NBA right away Davis went to Europe for three seasons. While overseas Davis played for teams in Italy and Greece, honing the skills that would make him one of the NBA's most valuable bench players.

Using those skills, Davis finally arrived in the league in '93 with authority, using his big, athletic body to block shots and rebound as a dominator of the paint. "I was really happy when Antonio came to our team, because combined with Dale [Davis] he took care of all the hard work for our team," says ex-Pacer and current 76er coach Larry Brown.

Today, just as the Pacers have become a complete team with realistic title aspirations, Davis has become a complete player. He has a jumper who's reliable from anywhere inside of 18 feet, and his athleticism makes face-adjusting jams a nightly occurrence. And of course, he's never forgotten his hard-working roots.

Stat Attack   Career Highlights

Born:	October 31, 1968, Oakland, CA	1990	Showed the makings of a great defender by being named Western Athletic Conference Defensive Player of the Year as a college senior
Ht/Wt:	6—9, 230 pounds		
School:	University of Texas El Paso	1994	Scored a team-high 26 points in his first-ever NBA start
Pro Career:	Indiana Pacers (1993–)	1994	Led all NBA rookies in rebounding (6.2 apg)
Career Avgs:	9.0 ppg, 6.6 rpg, 0.7 apg	1998	Ended the '97–98 season having played in 264 straight games, the best streak on the Pacers
		1999	Played in his fourth Eastern Conference Finals with the Pacers

BRIAN GRANT

Portland TrailBlazers

$5,000,000 42=

I t's no accident that the Portland TrailBlazers have become a Western Conference power in the two years that Brian Grant has been around. The passionate Grant can be that positive an influence on teams. With his long dreadlocks, massive Bob Marley tattoo and consistent performing of good deeds off the court, Grant's attitude belies the way he actually plays.

Unlike the thoughtful and peaceful man that Grant is, he is an extremely aggressive player. Much like he did in Sacramento when he played with Mitch Richmond, on a Portland team filled with scorers like Isaiah Rider and Damon Stoudamire, Grant is the guy who does the dirty work for the Blazers, scooping up rebounds and banging bodies in the low-post.

"He's the hardest-working guy in the league. You've gotta respect a cat like that," says Spurs center Tim Duncan.

Before Grant and the Blazers got to Duncan in the '99 Playoffs they had to beat the Jazz, and their power forward Karl Malone. Throughout the series, Grant neutralized the future Hall of Famer; and when the Blazers won the series, Grant got most of the credit. He'd earned it.

Stat Attack | Career Highlights

Born:	March 5, 1972, Columbus, OH	1994	Drafted in first round by the Sacramento Kings
Ht/Wt:	6—9, 254 pounds	1995	Named to the NBA All-Rookie First Team
School:	Xavier University		
Pro Career:	Sacramento Kings (1994–1997), Portland TrailBlazers (1997–)	1996	Ranked second on Kings in scoring (14.4 ppg) and rebounding (7.0 rpg)
		1997	Scored a career-high 34 points against the Suns
Career Avgs:	12.8 ppg, 7.9 rpg, 1.4 apg	1999	Named the winner of the J. Walter Kennedy Citizenship Award for his community service work

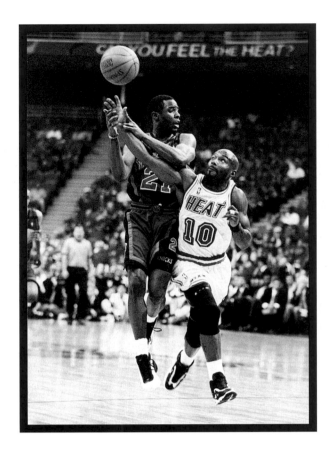

TIM HARDAWAY

Miami Heat

$4,800,000   44

Tim Hardaway may be short, and he may have suffered a career-threatening knee injury a few years back, but don't ever sleep on him. Hardaway is an assassin, needing only an inch of shooting space to make back-breaking three-pointers or breaking ankles with his cross-over dribble, which is the league's best.

More so than most, Hardaway's game is a product of his environment. Growing up in Chicago Hardaway played the outdoor game, but adjustments were needed for success. Regular jumpers got lost in the wind, so Hardaway created a unique game. He developed a jump shot with no rotation, a line drive less susceptible to the wind. His ugly, knuckling shot remains. Since even his unique shot wasn't a likely make on the playgrounds, Tim learned how to get to the basket on anyone. Hence the ill cross-over.

"Tim is unbelieveably hard to guard," says current Net Eric Murdock. "He'll hurt you with the crossover or back up and shoot it. He's one of those guys that can score so many ways." Hardaway complements his knack for scoring with an incredible determination to win. A tough combination, no matter what size he is.

Stat Attack

Born:	September 1, 1966, Chicago, IL
Ht/Wt:	6—0, 195 pounds
School:	University of Texas-El Paso
Pro Career:	Golden State Warriors (1989–96), Miami Heat (1996–)
Career Avgs:	19.4 ppg, 3.6 rpg, 9.0 apg

Career Highlights

1990	Chosen unanimously for the NBA All-Rookie First Team after averaging a team-high 8.7 apg
1993	Averaged more than 20 ppg and 10 apg for the second straight season
1997	Scored a career-high 45 points against the Wizards
1998	Appeared in his fifth career All-Star game
1999	Selected for the 1999 US Men's basketball team which will attempt to qualify for the 2000 Olympics

DOUG CHRISTIE

Toronto Raptors

$4,750,000   45

Doug Christie and the Toronto Raptors are the perfect fit of player and team. Christie entered the league after playing against mediocre competition for Pepperdine, and while he had loads of physical talent his game needed a lot of polish. Needless to say, impatient NBA towns like L.A. and New York are not where you polish your game, and throughout Christie's first three and a half seasons he spent as much time on the bench as he did on the court. In '96, however, Christie got traded to the neophyte Raptors, whose franchise history consisted of a whopping 50 games.

Toronto was a place Christie could learn the nuances of the game, and Toronto was happy to be patient, and with good reason. By year two with TO, Christie had developed into a bona fide NBA two-guard with better-than-average scoring ability and killer instincts on defense, where he took on the likes of Michael Jordan and Reggie Miller with gusto. "It's obvious that Doug had the physical tools," says Isaiah Thomas, the Raptor's former GM. "He just needed someone to have confidence in him. We did, and it paid off."

A happy marriage through and through.

Stat Attack   Career Highlights

Born:	May 9, 1970, Seattle, WA
Ht/Wt:	6—6, 205 pounds
School:	Pepperdine
Pro Career:	Seattle SuperSonics (1992–93), Los Angeles Lakers (1993–94), New York Knicks (1994–96), Toronto Raptors (1996–)
Career Avgs:	12.3 ppg, 4.1 rpg, 3.0 apg

1992 Seattle native was chosen 17th overall by his hometown team in the NBA Draft

1996 Traded from New York to Toronto, where he'd finally get a chance to play

1997 Recorded a career-high and Raptors franchise-record nine steals against the Nuggets

1998 Led the Raptors in steals and finished third in the NBA, with 2.44 spg

1999 Played in every one of his team's games for the first time as a pro

TONI KUKOC
Chicago Bulls

$4,560,000 | 46

I t is undeniable that Toni Kukoc's career has been a success. It is equally undeniable that it has not met the expectations both he and the Bulls had — at least not yet. For a few years, while Kukoc was dominating European basketball, he was the apple of Bulls GM Jerry Krause's eye. Krause tirelessly courted Kukoc, offering money and the chance to play with MJ. Well, Kukoc finally took Krause up on his offer and came over before the '93—94 season. Problem was, Jordan had surprisingly moved into retirement number one; and while Kukoc got his payday, underpaid Scottie Pippen was envious and treated Kukoc like dirt. After a year and a half away from the game Jordan returned, but he hardly embraced Kukoc. This past winter Jordan walked away from the game again, leaving Kukoc with three cherished championships, but not much respect. "Toni always had the ability, but he's been in the middle of a lot of battles on this team, and that has to affect a guy," said Steve Kerr last season.

In '99 Kukoc led a Bulls team that had no Jordan or Pippen, and he didn't do all that well. The intrigue continues...

Stat Attack

Born:	September 18, 1968, Split, Croatia
Ht/Wt:	6—11, 232 pounds
School:	N/A
Pro Career:	Chicago Bulls (1993–)
Career Avgs:	13.9 ppg

Career Highlights

1993	A three-time European Player of the Year, Kukoc finally made his long-awaited Bull debut
1994	Named to the NBA All-Rookie First Team
1996	Dropped a career-high 34 points on the Miami Heat
1996	Named NBA Sixth Man of the Year for his fine play off the bench
1998	Won his third straight NBA Title as a Chicago Bull

JAMAL
MASHBURN
Miami Heat

$4,400,000 | 47=

Thankfully for both Jamal Mashburn and his fans, the man is still only 26 years old. If you'd watched his career, from New York City high school prodigy through college star at Kentucky to All-Rookie performer for the Dallas Mavericks all the way to oft-injured member of the Miami Heat, you'd swear that Mash was pushing 30.

Mashburn has really been around the league for six seasons, missing major portions of three with a variety of injuries. When he hasn't been hurt, Mash has shown a skilled — if a tad one-dimensional — game that emphasizes scoring. Listen to former Maverick teammate and current Milwaukee Buck Chris Gatling describe the myriad ways that Mash can hurt the opposition: "He's got a world of talent. He can put the ball on the floor, shoot the three. Plus, he's a hard worker, a go-to guy that you can always count on down the stretch, and he'll give it you every night."

Well, at least every night that he's not hurt. If Pat Riley can just get him in top shape, the Mashburn we see in Y2K may be the one that's been envisioned for years. He is, after all, still just 26.

Stat Attack

Born:	November 29, 1972, New York, NY
Ht/Wt:	6—8, 241 pounds
School:	University of Kentucky
Pro Career:	Dallas Mavericks (1993–1997), Miami Heat (1997–)
Career Avgs:	18.1 ppg, 4.6 rpg, 3.2 apg

Career Highlights

1993	Led the Kentucky Wildcats to the Final Four during his junior season at Kentucky
1993	Selected in the first round by the Dallas Mavericks
1994	Named to the NBA All-Rookie First Team after tying for the Mavs' team scoring lead at 19.2 ppg
1995	Ended the '94–95 season with a career-high 24.1 ppg average
1999	After missing the first half of the season with a knee injury, came back to help the Heat to the Atlantic Division Championship

KENDALL GILL

New Jersey Nets

$4,400,000 47=

Fast, agile and graceful, Kendall Gill often looks like he should be playing soccer or even dancing rather than hooping it up. Not that his finesse-based skills have hurt Gill that much. Ever since he started making noises with a University of Illinois team that reached the Final Four in 1990, Gill has been a solid — and occasionally spectacular — pro.

During his immediate post-college years in Charlotte, Gill progressed nicely, but his career hit a bump during his two-year stay in Seattle. Playing for cantankerous coach George Karl, the sensitive Gill had his problems, but he was eventually re-routed back to Charlotte and regained his fine form.

Gill's pro career reached its peak in '97, when he combined his athleticism with a stable mid-range jumper to average a career-high 21.8 ppg for the Nets. It looked like Gill had really arrived as a player, but then the Nets up and traded him for rookie sensation Keith Van Horn, and Gill was pushed out of the spotlight again. Not that he struggled adjusting. "Kendall Gill is a true professional," says ex-Net coach John Calipari. "When we needed points he'd get them, but he'd do all the other things to help us as well."

Stat Attack

Born:	May 25, 1968, Chicago, IL
Ht/ Wt:	6—5, 216 pounds
School:	University of Illinois
Pro Career:	Charlotte Hornets (1990–93), Seattle SuperSonics (1993–95), Hornets (1995–96), New Jersey Nets (1996–)
Career Avgs:	15.5 ppg, 4.6 rpg, 3.5 apg, 1.8 spg

Career Highlights

1990	Selected fifth overall in the NBA Draft by the Charlotte Hornets
1991	Set Hornets' rookie records for highest free-throw percentage (.835), most assists (303) and steals (104) in a season
1991	Named to the NBA All-Rookie First Team
1996	One of only three players to score in double figures in all 82 games, highlighted by a career-high 41 points against the Orlando Magic
1997	Led the Nets in scoring with a career-high 21.8 ppg average

OTIS THORPE

Washington Wizards

$4,400,000 **47=**

To realize fully just how long Otis Thorpe has been around, and just how effective he's been, consider this: when his streak of 542 consecutive games played ended, it was only 1992. OT has been putting in good work for seven years since then, and that is no joke.

Despite standing 6—10, Thorpe is actually quite thin, but that hasn't stopped him from a lengthy career at power forward, the position usually manned by the league's big brutes. To grab rebounds or complete lay-ups among the wide bodies, Thorpe has used his lithe frame and his basketball knowledge to find a way. And in the process, old Otis has been able to impact the game's future as well.

'Otis is like a coach for us," says Wizards GM Wes Unseld. "We think he's a great influence on the younger players."

Thorpe was a free agent in the summer of 1999 and, with the Wizards seemingly eons away from a possible title, Thorpe may take his show to a place he might win another ring. For whoever signs him, it's like a two-for-one deal; the man can coach and play.

Stat Attack   Career Highlights

Born:	August 5, 1962, Boynton Beach, FL
Ht/Wt:	6—10, 246 pounds
School:	Providence College
Pro Career:	Sacramento Kings (1984–88), Houston Rockets (1989–94), Portland Trailblazers (1994–95), Detroit Pistons (1995–97), Kings (1997–98), Vancouver Grizzlies (1998), Washington Wizards (1999–)
Career Avgs:	14.9 ppg, 8.7 rpg, 2.3 apg

1984 Named to the NBA All-Rookie First Team after averaging 12.8 ppg and 6.8 rpg for the Sacramento Kings

1992 Selected as an NBA All-Star

1992 His streak of 542 consecutive games played in came to an end — a streak which remains the 13th-longest in NBA history

1994 Started at forward for NBA champions Houston Rockets

1999 Scored his 17,000th career point

1999 Grabbed his 10,000th career rebound

VIN BAKER

Seattle SuperSonics

$4,300,000 | 50

Despite a relatively down year in '99, Vin Baker enters free agency in the summer of '99 for the first time in his career, and is guaranteed a fat payday. The fact is, few players can bring the offense and rebounding that this big man can on a consistent basis. And there's no reason Baker can't bounce back from his one bad season.

During the long and ugly lockout of '98, some players stayed in tip-top shape. Baker was, unfortunately, one of the ones that didn't. As a result, when play resumed, he played passively and then got hurt. But all he has to do is forget about it; a lot of his fans will. And if he recaptures the form that he displayed in Milwaukee and during his first year in Seattle, it'll be watch out, league. Baker is a perfect power forward, capable of doing his man with a crafty move on the blocks, or taking him outside to school him with a J.

Ex team-mate Eric Snow sure thinks that Bake is valuable. "We called him 'the Truth,' because every time we needed a big game or a game-winning shot from him, he came through with it."

Stat Attack   Career Highlights

Born:	November 23, 1971, Lake Wales, FL	1994	Drafted in the first round by the Milwaukee Bucks
Ht/ Wt:	6—11, 250 pounds	1995	Selected to the NBA All-Rookie First Team
School:	University of Hartford	1995	Recorded his first career triple-double with 12 points, 12 rebounds and 12 assists against the Charlotte Hornets
Pro Career:	Milwaukee Bucks (1993–1997), Seattle SuperSonics (1997–)	1997	Named to the All-NBA Third Team
		1998	Named to his fourth career All-Star Game
Career Avgs:	18.1 ppg, 9.0 rpg, 2.5 apg	1999	Selected for the 1999 USA Men's Senior team

Born:	March 12, 1971, Oakland, CA	1993	Named to the NBA All-Rookie First Team after an outstanding season in which he averaged 16.6 ppg and 4.0 rpg
Ht/Wt:	6—5, 215 pounds		
School:	University of Nevada at Las Vegas	1994	Won the NBA Slam-Dunk Contest held during the NBA All-Star Weekend in Minneapolis
Pro Career:	Minnesota Timberwolves (1993–1996), Portland TrailBlazers (1996–)	1995	Scored a career-high 42 points against the Warriors
		1996	Tallied a Blazers season-high 40 points against the Celtics
Career Avgs:	18.0 ppg, 4.0 rpg, 2.8 apg	1998	Blazer's leading scorer at 19.7 ppg, which was also 15th overall in the league

ISAIAH RIDER
Portland TrailBlazers

$4,210,000   51

I saiah "JR" Rider is a notorious figure. And in more ways than one. Rider is certainly infamous — a string of traffic incidents, missed practices and league suspensions have ensured that. But he's also well-known for his game. JR may be an absolute gunner who has been known to treat passing as if it's a disease, but the man has always been able to shoot the rock.

And when he's not dropping bombs from the outside, Rider has wowed fans with his ill dunks. The highlight of the Oakland native's dunking career was the '95 Slam-Dunk Contest which Rider won with his patented "East Bay Funk" dunk, electrifying the fans in Minnesota, where he played at the time.

"Isaiah Rider is nasty," says teammate Greg Anthony. "And I mean that in the good way."

In '99, Rider actually dropped some of his bad nastiness, and gleefully took part in the remarkable team effort that brought the TrailBlazers to the Western Conference Finals. He even turned into somewhat of a media darling, catching rave reviews for his unselfish and clutch play. If Rider doesn't do something soon, his notoriety may start to be all positive.

DARRELL ARMSTRONG

Orlando Magic

$4,200,000 | 52

There are circuitous routes to the NBA. Then there's the route Darrell Armstrong took. Before DA reached the Orlando Magic, he had played in leagues most fans have never even heard of: besides the CBA, there was the United States Basketball League and the Global Basketball Association, as well as stints in Spain and Cyprus.

Throughout Armstrong's wild ride around the world, all he ever wanted was a chance to show the NBA that he was good enough to play in it. The Magic finally gave it to him in 1994, and Armstrong never looked back. Armstrong is a perfect model for people in all walks of life who want to quit. "Darrell has made it to the NBA because of his competitive nature," says his college coach, Jeff Capel. "He had some talent, but I didn't think he had enough to do better than make it to a pro level overseas. But he wanted to make it to the NBA so badly."

In 1999, Darrell Armstrong did a lot more than just show he deserved to be in the league. He darn near dominated it at times. Playing at a speed that most players either don't have or hesitate to use, DA was a dynamo all season, sparking the Magic to victories with his spirit.

Stat Attack

Born:	June 22, 1968, Gastonia, NC
Ht/Wt:	6—1, 185 pounds
School:	Fayetteville State
Pro Career:	Orlando Magic (1994–)
Career Avgs:	8.8 ppg, 2.3 rpg, 4.2 apg

Career Highlights

1990	Known as "Sky" at the time, won the CIAA Slam-Dunk Contest
1994	Signed to a 10-day contract with the Orlando Magic
1995	Re-signed by the Magic to first real contract
1999	Twice scored a a career-high 28 points
1999	Won an unprecedented two awards: NBA Most Improved Player and NBA Sixth Man of the Year

Born:	March 19, 1968, Cincinnatti, OH
Ht/Wt:	6—9, 250 pounds
School:	Xavier University
Pro Career:	Golden State Warriors (1990–93) Cleveland Cavaliers (1993–1997), Milwaukee Bucks (1997–1999), Philadelphia 76ers (1999–)
Career Avgs:	9.6 ppg, 8.5 rpg, 0.8 apg

1992 — Warriors' leading rebounder with 10.2 rpg

1995 — Played in his first All-Star Game, snaring four rebounds in front of his hometown fans in Cleveland

1995 — Totaled career-best 13.8 ppg and 10.9 rpg, which was fifth best in the league

1996 — Established a Cavs single-season franchise record by shooting 60% from the field

1998 — Grabbed a career-best 20 rebounds and added 10 points against the Los Angeles Lakers

TYRONE HILL
Philadelphia
76ers

$4,110,000   53

Tyrone Hill carries a scowl, and is best known for his not-so-sunny disposition. But since he's a basketball player, this is a good thing. If the League were filled with happy-go-lucky scorers who didn't want to bump and grind, what fun would that be?

So in the realistic, late-'90s NBA, the one dominated by intense defense and all-out wars underneath the glass, Hill is the man you want. All arms and angles as he chases down another board, Hill has no second thoughts about, say, misplacing an elbow in an opponent's mid-section. But it's not just dirty stuff that T-Time has picked up during his long career. Just ask ex-teammate Glenn Robinson: "He taught me a lot out there. How to step in the lane and get steals, how to pick up guys off screens, and just how to go out there prepared every single night."

Hill was dealt from Milwaukee to Philadelphia midway through the '99 season, and picked up where he'd left off, serving as Allen Iverson's bodyguard and as the team's dirty work-doer. Not coincidentally, the 76ers had some Playoff success. Remember, a good NBA team needs the glitz and the grime.

Born:	March 26, 1962, Spokane, WA
Ht/Wt:	6—1, 175 pounds
School:	Gonzaga University
Pro Career:	Utah Jazz (1984–)
Career Avgs:	13.4 ppg, 11.1 apg, 2.7 rpg, 2.3 spg

1984	Selected by the Utah Jazz in the first round of the NBA Draft
1987	Led the NBA in assists with 13.8 apg for the first of what would be an NBA-record nine consecutive seasons
1990	Averaged an all-time NBA high of 14.5 assists per game
1991	Served up a career-high 28 assists versus the Bucks
1995	Became the NBA's career leader in assists, passing Magic Johnson
1996	Broke Maurice Cheeks' record of 2,310 steals to become the NBA's career leader in steals
1998	Scored his 15,000th career point
1998	Appeared in the NBA Finals for the second consecutive season
1999	Grabbed his 3,000th career rebound

JOHN STOCKTON

Utah Jazz

$4,000,000 | 54=

There have certainly been point guards who can score a lot better than John Stockton, but is that even in their job description? A true point guard should worry about two things: passing the ball and defending his man. John Stockton only does those things better than any player in NBA history. This is no hyperbole. Stockton is the runaway career NBA leader in assists and steals, and at age 37 he's still going strong.

Almost as remarkable as all that Stockton has accomplished is the way in which he's done it. No big contracts, no advertisements, no controversies. This guy doesn't even have an agent. To recap: John Stockton's statistical achievements are the most unique in NBA history, and he may be the most modest player in NBA history.

"John Stockton does all the things that separate the great players from the good ones. He's a great decision-maker, always knowing when to pass or when to shoot, and he's also willing to sacrifice his body on offense and defense," says Jazz President Frank Layden. One thing's for certain: there aren't many other players who fit that description — and Layden didn't even mention Stock's simple wardrobe.

Stat Attack

Born:	November 14, 1970, San Antonio, TX
Ht/Wt:	6—1, 202 pounds
School:	Baylor University
Pro Career:	New Jersey Nets (1993–94), Boston Celtics (1994–97), Charlotte Hornets (1997–)
Career Avgs:	11.5 ppg, 5.4 apg, 2.7 rpg

Career Highlights

1993	Signed as a free agent with the Nets after being named to the Continental Basketball Association All-Rookie First Team
1995	Twice equaled the Celtics' record for three-pointers in a game with seven, both times against the Hornets
1996	Played in all 82 games of the season, the only Celtic player to do so
1997	Scored 21 points in the first quarter, establishing a Hornets franchise record, and ended up tallying a season-high 32 points against the Houston Rockets
1998	Led the Hornets in assists and steals with 6.5 apg and 1.73 spg respectively

DAVID WESLEY

Charlotte Hornets

$4,000,000   54=

Completely unheralded when he came out of Baylor University, David Wesley has made a career for himself with rugged point guard play, most recently with the Charlotte Hornets. There may be a good reason why Wesley didn't attract much attention after college: his body doesn't seem fit to be anywhere near a basketball court. Wesley's got a big, barrel-like chest, and he's rumored to push massive Charlotte teammate Anthony Mason in the weightroom. But at only 6—1, you wouldn't even picture Wesley playing American football.

But while people were looking at Wesley's weird build or unspectacular college pedigree, DW was busting his ass, working on all facets of his game. And when he did get a chance, first with the Nets and then with the Celtics, Wesley made the most of it. Wesley's run in Boston showed that he was ready to be taken seriously as a player. Charlotte came with the loot, and Wesley became a Hornet, which made his teammates awfully happy.

"People like David Wesley don't get any respect in this league," says Mason. "And why? Because he wasn't a first-round draft pick? Come on. The guy could play, and he's a good leader."

Born:	November 20, 1967, Bakersfield, CA	1994	Signed with the New Jersey Nets after earning CBA Most Valuable Player honors
Ht/Wt:	6—3, 195 pounds	1996	Scored 20 points to go along with his career-high 17 assists against the Lakers
School:	Boise State University		
Pro Career:	New Jersey Nets (1994–96), New York Knicks (1996–)	1996	Recorded his first career triple-double, scoring 18 points, dishing out 14 assists and grabbing 10 rebounds against the Chicago Bulls
Career Avgs:	8.6ppg, 5.2 apg, 1.0 spg	1996	Named the Nets' MVP after averaging career-bests of 12.8 ppg, 7.0 apg and 1.4 spg during the 1995–96 season
		1997	Notched his 1,000th career assist

CHRIS CHILDS

New York Knicks

$4,000,000 **54=**

With a bad alcohol problem and a worse temper, one-time Bosie State star Chris Childs seemed to be the perfect player for the CBA. High on talent and low on basketball brains, most scouts figured Childs would spend his career languishing in the minor leagues, bitching at refs and throwing stupid passes while his considerable skills went to waste.

But then Childs made a change. More than six years ago, Childs kicked the alcohol habit. And after an MVP season in the CBA in '94, the New Jersey Nets came calling. It took a while for Double-C to get used to the way things get done in the league but Childs was patient, ultimately playing Kenny Anderson right out of New Jersey.

Having proved that he belonged, Childs jumped at a six-year, $24-million contract offer from the Knicks. To the Knicks' chagrin, Childs relapsed in '98. Not into substance abuse, but into basketball abuse. The decision-making skills people thought he'd learned for good were gone. '99 brought back the Childs that starred in New Jersey, however, and by season's end he was a Knick that coach Jeff Van Gundy trusted. "I have a lot of faith in Chris Childs, and he's earned it by making big plays for our team," said Van Gundy.

Born:	March 25, 1969, Toccoa, GA	1991	Selected by Pacers in the first round of the NBA Draft
Ht/Wt:	6—11, 230 pounds	1992	Set a Pacers single-season franchise record with a .568 field-goal percentage
School:	Clemson University	1993	Tied a franchise record with 12 offensive rebounds against the San Antonio Spurs
Pro Career:	Indiana Pacers (1991–)	1994	Established a career high in scoring by netting 28 points against the Washington Bullets
Career Avgs:	9.3 ppg, 8.8 rpg, 1.36 bpg	1998	Led the Pacers in field-goal percentage for the fourth consecutive season (55%) and rebounds for the fifth consecutive year (7.8 rpg)
		1998	Ended the season as the Pacers' career leader in field-goal percentage, knocking down .550 of his attempts during his career

DALE DAVIS

Indiana Pacers

$4,000,000 54=

Despite being the worst free throw shooter in NBA History, Dale Davis has found a number of other ways to be an effective player. For the most part, those ways have been absolutely tireless work on the glass, as well as the ability to dunk the ball on anyone and block shots with a violent ferocity. These are the skills that Davis has shown ever since he intimidated the opposition in the ACC when he played for Clemson University; and with a body that seems to have been chiseled out of stone, it was no surprise that Davis was a banger on the court.

What is a mild surprise is the way Davis carries himself off the court. More like a big teddy bear than the thug he plays on TV, Davis is a soft-spoken cat who devotes much of his time to children's causes. Davis pays the way for youngsters from both Indianapolis as well as his native Toccoa, GA to attend his basketball camp, and he's put more than a few students through college. DD also runs a clothing shop with teammate Mark Jackson.

"Dale does it all," Jackson says. "We know we can count on him on and off the court."

P.J. BROWN
Miami Heat

$4,000,000   54=

Having established himself as a hard-working combo forward throughout a three-year career with the New Jersey Nets, P.J. Brown entered the '96 off-season as a free agent. Observers around the league figured he'd simply remain with the Nets as an averagely-paid, averagely-talented player. Then Pat Riley stepped in, offering a rich, long-term deal that shocked the Nets. Brown accepted, and has gone on to prove that he may be worth every penny.

Playing for Riley requires sacrifice of the highest order. Players must practice card and play even harder; diving for loose balls is not nodded at — it's expected. Luckily for Heat fans, Brown does all those things. On top of the hustle, Brown has also developed a little bit of an offensive game, now capable of hitting his awkward-looking shot from all around the perimeter. Proof of Brown's growth has come in the last couple of seasons: whenever teams talk trades with Riley, Brown's name invariably comes up, and Riley invariably says no. At one point, calling Brown untouchable would have seemed silly. Now it seems logical. "P.J.'s a warrior. He'll play hard no matter what the circumstances," says teammate Alonzo Mourning.

Stat Attack

Born:	October 14, 1969, Detroit, MI
Ht/Wt:	6—11, 240 pounds
School:	Louisiana Tech
Pro Career:	New Jersey Nets (1993–96), Miami Heat (1996–)
Career Avgs:	9.1 ppg, 7.2 rpg, 1.3 bpg

Career Highlights

1994	Took part in the Schick Rookie Game during the All-Star Weekend in Minneapolis
1996	Established a career high with 30 points against the Toronto Raptors
1997	Selected to the NBA All-Defensive Second Team
1997	Won the J. Walter Kennedy Citizenship Award, the league's finest off-court honor
1998	Snared a career-high 20 rebounds against the L.A. Clippers
1999	An integral part of the Miami Heat's Atlantic Division Championship team

DONYELL MARSHALL
Golden State Warriors

$3,990,000 | 59

For a long while, Donyell Marshall had "bust" written all over him. When you're drafted fourth in the NBA Draft — as Marshall was — you should be counting your All-Star appearances once you've been around for four seasons. Instead, all Marshall was counting was splinters in his ass. Things didn't start out that bad. Playing for the young Timberwolves for much of his rookie year, Marshall dropped nearly 13 ppg and was seen as a future star. But when he got traded to Golden State and planted firmly on the depth chart behind future Hall of Famer Chris Mullin, things stared to go downhill fast. In the '96–97 season, there were 18 games in which Marshall didn't play. Nary a second, and never because of injury. This was tragic for a silky-smooth forward with a world of skills.

Before the '97–98 season, however, Mullin got traded and the Warriors brought in a new coach. A fresh start for Marshall, and fresh results as well. Suddenly the league saw the guy they'd expected a few years back. "It was gonna happen sooner or later," teammate Bimbo Coles says of Marshall's rebirth. "He just had a lot of obstacles to overcome, but now he's playing the way he's capable of playing."

Stat Attack

Born:	May 18, 1973, Reading, PA
Ht/Wt:	6—9, 230 pounds
School:	University of Connecticut
Pro Career:	Minnesota Timberwolves (1994–95), Golden State Warriors (1995–)
Career Avgs:	10.6 ppg, 5.9 rpg, 1.4 apg

Career Highlights

1994	Selected by the Timberwolves with the fourth pick in the NBA Draft
1994	Established career highs of 30 points and 13 rebounds in his first start in the league
1995	Scored 11 points in the Schick Rookie Game during All-Star Weekend in Phoenix
1995	Named to the NBA All-Rookie Second Team
1998	Tallied career bests in scoring (15.4 ppg), rebounds (8.6 rpg) and assists (2.2 apg) over the course of the 1997–98 season

WALT WILLIAMS

Portland Trailblazers

$3,750,000 | 60=

N icknamed "The Wizard" during his halcyon days at the University of Maryland, Walt Williams has earned the nickname both with his mystical on-court play as well as for the way he has continuously reinvented himself as a player.

On the court, Williams can do it all. Earvin Johnson may have been "magical," as a 6—9 point guard, but Williams has similar skills. Sporting his high socks and dated 'do, the 6—8 Williams is capable of confounding opponents that don't know what to expect. Williams can give you a playground crossover and take you to the hoop; a straight-up three-point shot from 24 feet out; or even a no-look bounce pass for an assist. Knowing Williams is at least capable of so many wondrous things on a basketball court, you may wonder why he is not really one of the NBA's premier players. Well, he's been victimized by injuries and he's been with four different teams. This has been chaotic, but he's always adjusted. In college Williams played point, then with Sacramento he was a shooting guard and in the years since he's been a designated three-point shooter or sixth man. "Walt has been put in some tough situations, but he always handles himself as a professional, and we feel lucky to have him," says Blazers coach Mike Dunleavy.

Stat Attack

Born:	April 16, 1970, Washington, DC
Ht/Wt:	6—8, 230 pounds
School:	University of Maryland
Pro Career:	Sacramento Kings (1992–95), Miami Heat (1995–96), Toronto Raptors (1996–97), Portland Trailblazers (1997–)
Career Avgs:	13.8 ppg, 4.2 rpg, 2.8 apg

Career Highlights

1992	Selected in the first round of the NBA Draft by the Sacramento Kings after a dazzling career at the University of Maryland
1993	Scored a career-high 40 points as a rookie against the Philadelphia 76ers
1993	Named to the NBA All-Rookie Second Team
1997	Established career-highs in rebounds (5.0 rpg), three-pointers made and threes attempted
1997	Took part in the NBA Three-Point Contest during the All-Star Weekend

CLIFFORD ROBINSON

Phoenix Suns

$3,750,000   60=

Stat Attack	Career Highlights

Born:	December 16, 1966, Albion, NY
Ht/Wt:	6—10, 225 pounds
School:	University of Connecticut
Pro Career:	Portland Trailblazers (1989–97), Phoenix Suns (1997–)
Career Avgs:	16.0 ppg, 5.2 rpg, 2.1 apg

1989	Picked by the Portland Trailblazers in the first round of the NBA draft after an acclaimed career at the University of Connecticut
1990	Opened his career with a streak of 461 consecutive games played, still the longest streak in Blazers history
1993	Won the NBA Sixth Man Award, having averaged 19.1 ppg and 6.6 rpg
1994	Named to his first NBA All-Star Game
1996	On July 1, netted a career-high 41 points against the Minnesota Timberwolves while being named the NBA's Player of the Week
1997	Scored his 10,000th career point

Cliff Robinson enters the '99 offseason as a free agent whom Phoenix must retain. Not only are the Suns expected to keep Robinson in the fold, but they're also going to pay him quite handsomely — even more than he has been in the past.

The reason for Robinson's value lies in his defensive skills. If you followed Robinson as a somewhat-flaky, offensive-minded, headband-wearing youngster in college and throughout his first few years in the NBA, you may be shocked that CR is now associated with the unglamorous side of ball, but that is what has happened.

Ever since Robinson has been in Phoenix he has maintained an offensive game that can hurt you from inside or out, but he's also become one of the game's most versatile defenders. "We can put Cliff on almost anyone," says Suns coach Danny Ainge. "If we need him to guard a two-guard, he'll do it, but he could also defend forwards and centers as well. That makes him an extremely valuable member of our team."

It cannot be understated how little was ever expected from Robinson as an NBA defender, but sometimes people really change. And Robinson is gonna get paid for his changes.

Born:	October 10, 1966	1988	Named to the NBA All-Rookie Team
Ht/Wt:	6—10, 225 pounds	1991	Scored 15.3 ppg to lead the Sonics in scoring
School:	University of Alabama	1995	Pacers leader in steals with 1.54 spg
Pro Career:	Seattle SuperSonics (1987–93), Indiana Pacers (1993–)	1996	Named to his second NBA All-Defensive Second Team
		1996	Recorded his 9,000th career point
Career Avgs:	12.4 ppg, 4.9 rpg, 2.6 apg		

DERRICK McKEY

Indiana Pacers

$3,600,000   62

A sinewy forward with a grab-bag of skills, Derrick McKey is the type of guy that will have a huge impact on a game without you even noticing. As his mediocre career digits indicate, McKey is not going to jump out of the boxscore with 37-point, 18-rebound-type nights. But what McKey does is all the little things that help his team win.

McKey is great at taking charges, grabbing loose balls, deflecting passes and tipping rebounds. If it's the type of play that helps a team and doesn't get much publicity, you can bet McKey has done it. Perhaps most impressive about McKey's approach to the game is that he doesn't necessarily have to be this way. Derrick possesses a nifty jumper and a steady variety of low-post moves, offensive skills that would ensure him a job even if he was scared to get grimy during the game. All that McKey does is noticed around the league. "Derrick McKey is a player that I'd like to be compared to," says Keith Van Horn of the Nets.

People who have seen Van Horn's offense-first game may laugh at that, but you have to respect Van Horn for thinking of McKey as a role model; he has earned that distinction.

Born:	May 3, 1963, LaGrange, IL
Ht/Wt:	6—4, 190 pounds
School:	Iowa State University
Pro Career:	Phoenix Suns (1986–92), Philadelphia 76ers (1992–93), Utah Jazz (1993–)
Career Avgs:	14.7 ppg, 3.5 rpg, apg, 1.47 spg

1986	Drafted by the Phoenix Suns
1991	Snared a career-high 14 rebounds
1992	Tallied 11 points in the NBA All-Star Game
1994	Established an NBA record by hitting eight consecutive three-pointers without a miss, while scoring a career-high 40 points against the Seattle SuperSonics
1995	Scored the 10,000th point of his career
1998	Won the NBA Three-Point Contest during All-Star Weekend in New York
1998	Appeared in his second straight NBA Final with the Jazz

JEFF HORNACEK
Utah Jazz

$3,500,000   63=

T he NBA is filled with dozens of electrifying players, guys that can leap high and seemingly never come down, dropping in jaw-dropping baskets while they're at it. Jeff Hornacek is NOT one of those players.

Hornacek's game is one of angles and guile, as he uses a court sense, a large dose of confidence and a knack for knocking down his jump shot to score for the Jazz. Some people look at Hornacek's bookish appearance and his normal build and label him a "throwback," as if the NBA in the 1960s featured cats that needed to throw up back-bending runners or double-pump leaners to get a shot off. But no, Hornacek is no throwback, he's just one of a kind.

Ask Jazz center Greg Foster about Hornacek, and you get an almost-mystified response: "The guy is incredible. He shoots the ball better than anyone I've ever seen. But it's not just his outside shot — he'll go to the hole and give you some schoolyard stuff, too."

For two straight NBA Finals, Hornacek was matched up with the Bulls' Michael Jordan, and never got embarrassed; that should tell you something about the guy.

Born:	August 17, 1969, Angola, NY
Ht/Wt:	6—11, 245 pounds
School:	Duke University
Pro Career:	Minnesota Timberwolves (1992–95), Atlanta Hawks (1995–98), Detroit Pistons (1999–)
Career Avgs:	16.3 ppg, 7.8 rpg, 2.9 apg

1992   Won his second national title with Duke University

1992   Selected in the first round of the NBA Draft by the Timberwolves (third overall)

1992   The lone collegiate member of the original "Dream Team" that won the gold medal at the 1992 Summer Olympics in Barcelona

1993   Led the Timberwolves in scoring and rebounding with 18.2 ppg and 8.7 rpg

1997   Scored 7 points and grabbed 11 rebounds in his first All-Star Game in Cleveland

1998   Finished ninth in the League in free-throw percentage at .864

CHRISTIAN LAETTNER

Detroit Pistons

$3,500,000   63=

While an Achilles injury suffered in the '98 offseason has pushed Christian Laettner out of the limelight for a bit you can bet he'll resurface, for there have been few basketball players who can elicit the type of emotional response that Laettner can.

Laettner burst to the forefront while he starred for Duke, showing off a penchant for hitting big shots (Kentucky fans will forever vilify him for the shot he hit to knock the UK out of the '92 NCAA Tournament), but also showing a petulant side (he once stepped directly on a fallen player's chest.)

In the NBA, Laettner has done the same type of stuff, just to a lesser degree. He has shown flashes of brilliance on the court, including a great All-Star season in '96–97, but he's also been a brat, alienating teammates in both Minnesota and Atlanta. "Christian has all the tools, but he wasn't always a great fit for our team," says Timberwolves GM Kevin McHale.

Now that Laettner has moved on to the Pistons, and dealt with injuries, perhaps he'll come back next year as a quiet, solid performer. But don't bet on it.

Born:	November 29, 1968, Jacksonville	1990	Selected in the first round of the NBA Draft by the Boston Celtics
Ht/Wt:	6—2, 185 pounds	1991	Won the Slam-Dunk Contest in Charlotte
School:	University of Jacksonville	1994	Netted a career-high 40 points to complement seven rebounds, five assists and four steals against the Chicago Bulls
Pro Career:	Boston Celtics (1990–1997), Toronto Raptors (1997–)	1995	Celtics' leader in three-pointers made and attempted
Career Avgs:	11.6 ppg, 2.7 rpg, 3.8 apg	1999	Dished out his 2,000th career assist

DEE BROWN

Toronto Raptors

$3,500,000   63=

An unknown out of college and then instantly famous after his unbelievable Slam-Dunk Contest victory in '91, the Dee Brown that patrols the perimeter in '99 has settled into that lucrative land of "solid NBA player."

When Brown, a Jacksonville native, was drafted out of his hometown school, Jacksonville University, plenty of eyebrows were raised. Then Brown came with the sickness halfway through his rookie year, when he pumped up his Reebok pumps before flying to an exhilarating Slam-Dunk Contest victory. Brown became an instant celebrity and one of Reebok's most famous pitchmen. Then injuries and inconsistency knocked him off the map. Since Brown has played for the youthful Toronto Raptors, however, he has developed an outside shot and a veteran presence. The dunks have been replaced by something a little more valuable, at least to his coach. "Paired with all the young guys we have, Dee has been a very valuable and steady member of our team," says Raptors coach Butch Carter.

Well, Reebok may not consider him all that valuable any more for shoe advertising, but hopefully Dee values a solid career a little more than just his 15 minutes of fame.

Born:	December 14, 1966, Miami, FL
Ht/Wt:	6—8, 250 pounds
School:	Tennessee State University
Pro Career:	New Jersey Nets (1989–90), Denver Nuggets (1990–91), New York Knicks (1991–96), Charlotte Hornets (1996–)
Career Avgs:	10.8 ppg, 8.3 rpg, 3.1 apg

1989 Finally got a chance in the NBA after averaging 29.9 ppg for Tulsa in the CBA

1994 Appeared in the NBA Finals with the Knicks

1995 Named the NBA Sixth Man of the Year

1996 NBA leader in minutes played (42.2)

1997 Tied a Hornets record by canning all 11 of his field-goal attempts in a game against the Orlando Magic

1998 Hornets leader for the second straight season in field-goal percentage (.509) and rebounds (10.2 rpg)

ANTHONY MASON

Charlotte Hornets

$3,470,000   66

Anthony Mason may have been born in Miami, but he moved to New York City shortly thereafter, and the evidence is in his game. Mase is a quintessential New York baller — a hot-headed, trash-talkin' menace, with a collection of skills that you'd normally need two or three NBA players combined to come up with.

Mason grew up a baseball player and a bright student, and so his large basketball talents went unhoned. An unheard-of career at Tennessee State taught him a little something about the game, but Mase was not at the top of any NBA scout's list of prospects. It was with his hometown team, the Knicks, that Mason finally got his chance to blow up. Playing for head coach Pat Riley, Mason was able to show his fire and desire on the Madison Square Garden floor. While Mason continued to grow as a player, his sometimes-surly attitude eventually got him shipped off to Charlotte, where he has impressed the organization with his heart. "He approaches the game only one way, and that's all out. He may get on the other guys sometimes, but only because he wants to win. I don't have a problem with that," says Hornets coach Paul Silas.

DANA BARROS

Boston Celtics

$3,400,000   67

Stat Attack		Career Highlights
Born:	April 13, 1967, Boston MA	**1989** Selected by the Seattle SuperSonics in the first round of the NBA Draft
Ht/Wt:	5—11, 163 pounds	**1992** Led the league in three-point percentage by knocking down 44% of his attempts
School:	Boston College	**1995** Selected an NBA All-Star
Pro Career:	Seattle SuperSonics (1989–93) Philadelphia 76ers (1993–95) Boston Celtics (1995–)	**1996** Established an NBA record by hitting at least one three-pointer in 89 straight games from December 23, 1994 to January 10, 1996
Career Avgs:	11.3 ppg, 1.9 rpg, 3.5 apg	**1998** Had a season-high 29 points along with a career-high seven steals against the Vancouver Grizzlies

Dana Barros is an example of how far players who master one aspect of the game can go. Despite an outstanding college career at Boston College, the undersized Barros went largely unappreciated as a SuperSonic throughout his first few years in the League. But when Barros got to Philadelphia, he unleashed a deadly three-point shot on unsuspecting opponents, hitting triples off the dribble like no player had ever done. At one point Barros made at least one three-pointer in 89 straight games, and even parlayed his three-point shooting into an All-Star selection in '95.

Now, the emphasis on Barros's long bombs is not meant to undermine his skills. As a Celtic, Barros has displayed a nice handle and a steady hand as a sometimes-starting point guard. And that type of play doesn't go unnoticed. "What we've asked of Dana is that he always be ready for us, and he's responded with some valuable minutes," says Celtics head coach Rick Pitino.

That may be true, but you can be sure that if Barros had never perfected his triple, he wouldn't be counted on for anything else.

DETLEF SCHREMPF
Seattle SuperSonics

$3,330,000 | 68

Detlef Schrempf may come from Germany, but thanks to an exchange program that allowed him to play basketball as a high school senior in Washington and his subsequent college career at U-Dub, Schrempf entered the NBA knowing the nuances of the American game. Schrempf can play both sides of the ball well, and he displays few of the stereotypes that have plagued certain Europeans who make it to the NBA. For the past six seasons it has been the SuperSonics that have benefited from Schrempf's abilities.

"For a coach, he's one of those guys that's easy," says former SuperSonics coach George Karl. "He makes a coach's job simple, and that's rare in this game. In all my years of coaching I've never experienced a more professional person."

As Schrempf entered the '99 offseason, all indications were that he would take his sensible professionalism to a new locale. It says here that a team close to a title would be wise to pick him up. Cagey veterans that can do a little bit of everything are often the players that can push a team to the top. Schrempf is just that type of player.

Stat Attack

Born:	January 21, 1963, Leverkusen, Germany
Ht/Wt:	6—10, 235 pounds
School:	University of Washington
Pro Career:	Dallas Mavericks (1985–89), Indiana Pacers (1989–93), Seattle SuperSonics (1993–)
Career Avgs:	14.6 ppg, 6.4 rpg, 3.5 apg

Career Highlights

1985	Taken by the Dallas Mavericks in the first round of the NBA Draft
1992	Won the NBA Sixth Man Award for the second straight season
1993	Finished the season as the only NBA player in the top 25 in scoring (19.1 ppg), rebounding (9.5 rpg) and assists (6.0 apg)
1995	Selected to the All-NBA Third Team
1996	Played in the NBA Finals with the Sonics
1997	Selected to his third All-Star Game, where he has averaged 7.7 ppg and 2.3 rpg over his career

TIM DUNCAN
San Antonio Spurs

$3,300,000   69

Stat Attack   Career Highlights

Born:	April 25, 1976, Saint Croix, Virgin Islands	1997	Consensus College Player of the Year after senior season at Wake Forest
		1997	Selected first pick of the Draft
Ht/Wt:	7—0, 248 pounds	1998	The only rookie selected to the All-Star Game
School:	Wake Forest University		
Pro Career:	San Antonio Spurs (1997–)	1998	Named the NBA's Player of the Week for the week ending March 1, 1998
Career Avgs:	21.3 ppg, 11.7 rpg, 2.6 apg	1998	Named the NBA Rookie of the Month for all six months of the season, only the third player to do so in history
		1998	Named the NBA's Rookie of the Year
		1999	Selected to participate with the 1999 USA basketball

The stakes for Tim Duncan have been clearly laid out: along with Allen Iverson, Duncan is the future of the league. An immensely skilled player with a perfect body and a mental approach that is so calm that he almost looks bored at times, Duncan has the potential to win the MVP Award at least three or four times. Duncan grew up in the Virgin Islands and, besides balling, TD got busy in the swimming pool, where he showed Olympian skills. That's somewhat appropriate to the Duncan of today, since he can devastate opponents like the butterfly stroke does arms. Much of Duncan's value can be attributed to the fact that he spent a full four years in college, properly developing his game.

"Throughout a game, Duncan may not look like he's doing much, but then you look up at the scoreboard and it's: Lakers 20, Duncan 22. He's got a lot of weapons. Too many." This was the reaction of Lakers forward Robert Horry after Duncan helped San Antonio dismantle Los Angeles in Round Two of the '99 Playoffs. Then TD led San Antonio to its first-ever NBA Championship. And remember, this is just the beginning.

MARK JACKSON
Indiana Pacers

$3,200,000 | 70

If you don't watch him closely, you'll think Mark Jackson is an easy player to figure out. "This guy can't play," you'd say. This negative reaction would be caused by his physical attributes, or lack thereof. A slow guy who hasn't dunked in a good six years, Jackson has nonetheless confounded all observers by using court smarts and uncanny passing ability to excel throughout his major college career and his historic run in the NBA.

The reason for "Action's" impact is a simple one — the man is the quintessential selfless point guard. Jackson has made conventional bounce passes, around-the-back dishes, no-look deliveries and everything in between, to the point where he has now compiled more than 7,900 assists, good for reaching the top five in NBA history. In a league filled with egocentric players bent on scoring no matter who or what stands in their way, Jax's old-school approach makes him an extremely popular teammate. "Everyone wants to play with Mark Jackson," says former St. John's and current Pacer teammate Chris Mullin. "You go around the league and guys are like, 'Man, I wanna play with Mark. Let me play with Mark. I like that guy.'" Any fan that pays close attention should too.

Stat Attack

Born:	April 1, 1965, Brooklyn, NY
Ht/Wt:	6—3, 185 pounds
School:	St. John's
Pro Career:	New York Knicks (1987–92), Los Angeles Clippers (1992–1994), Indiana Pacers (1994–1996), Denver Nuggets (1996–97), Pacers (1997–)
Career Avgs:	10.8 ppg, 4.1 rpg, 8.6 apg

Career Highlights

1987	Graduated from St. John's University as the school's all-time assist leader
1988	Named NBA Rookie of the Year
1988	Set NBA single-season rookie assist record with 868
1989	Named to his first and only All-Star Game
1992	Led the Knicks in assists for the fifth time in his five New York seasons
1997	Led the NBA assists by averaging a career high 11.4 apg
1998	Moved into fifth place on the NBA's all-time assist list

ALLEN IVERSON
Philadelphia 76ers

$3,130,000 | 71

Stat Attack	Career Highlights

Born:	June 7, 1975, Hampton, VA	1996	Selected by the 76ers with the first pick in the 1996 NBA Draft
Ht/Wt:	6—0, 165 pounds	1996	Netted 30 points in his NBA debut against the Milwaukee Bucks
School:	Georgetown University	1996	Named MVP of the Rookie Game held during the All-Star Weekend, scoring 19 and handing out nine assists
Pro Career:	Philadelphia 76ers (1996–)		
Career Avgs:	23.7 ppg, 4.1 rpg, 6.3 apg, 2.3 spg	1997	Tallied 40 points in five consecutive games to set a rookie record, including a career-high 50 against the Cleveland Cavaliers
		1999	Led the NBA in scoring with 26.8 ppg
		1999	Steered the 76ers to the second round of the Playoffs for the first time since 1991

If you want to consider Tim Duncan as the quiet, smooth-jazz future of the NBA, Allen Iverson is its loud, hip-hop torch bearer. In today's game there is no player that can capture the fans' imagination the way AI can.

Iverson's remarkable talents have a lot to do with his appeal. He is lightning-quick, and when you watch him play it often looks as if he goes at a different speed than the other dudes on the court. But as transcendent as his game is, Iverson is also a favorite for some personal traits. At 6—0 and 165, Iverson is no imposing figure. His build is like that of many men on the street, which only makes the crazy shots he hits that much more impressive. Plus he embraces the hip-hop images of today, sporting corn rows in his hair and baggy clothes. A lot of kids love Iverson for just these reasons. Don't ever expect Iverson to go corporate like Jordan, but AI does have his own signature shoe, and he has a six-year, $71 million contract which will kick in next season. "Allen Iverson is the real deal. I can only imagine what he'll be doing once he's been in the league for a while," says Reggie Miller.

Born:	October 23, 1975, Diamond Bar, CA	**1997**	Selected with the second overall pick in the NBA Draft by the New Jersey Nets
Ht/Wt:	6—10, 250 pounds	**1997**	Scored 17 points and snared 10 rebounds in the NBA Rookie Game during All-Star Weekend
School:	University of Utah	**1997**	Selected unanimously to the NBA All-Rookie First Team after averaging 19.7 ppg and 6.6 rpg
Pro Career:	New Jersey Nets (1997–)	**1999**	Scored a career-high 35 points against the Detroit Pistons
Career Avgs:	20.5 ppg, 7.4 rpg, 1.6 apg	**1999**	Went for four straight double-doubles from March 12 to 17, averaging 19.0 ppg and 12.3 rpg

KEITH VAN HORN

New Jersey Nets

$3,100,000   72=

Just two years after a stellar college career at the University of Utah, Keith Van Horn has become the crutch that the New Jersey Nets franchise is leaning on to carry it to respectability.

Van Horn may have the build of a classic power forward, but when he was in high school he played alongside Wilt Chamberlain's nephew as well as the son of former baseball great George Hendrick. Needless to say, all three of them were big, and Van Horn exhibited the ability to play "small." This early-life experience created a 6—10 man who can dribble, shoot, pass and score with remarkable fluidity.

Van Horn's abilities are such that he can even hurt his team. "We've got so much confidence in Keith that sometimes we start depending on him too much," says Nets center Jayson Williams. "When he misses a shot, it's like the sun didn't come up. We don't know what to do."

The Nets alleviated some of the pressure on Van Horn when they picked up Stephon Marbury midway through last season. Steph and Keith should prove to be a particularly difficult duo to stop. Not that Van Horn had any problems running things alone.

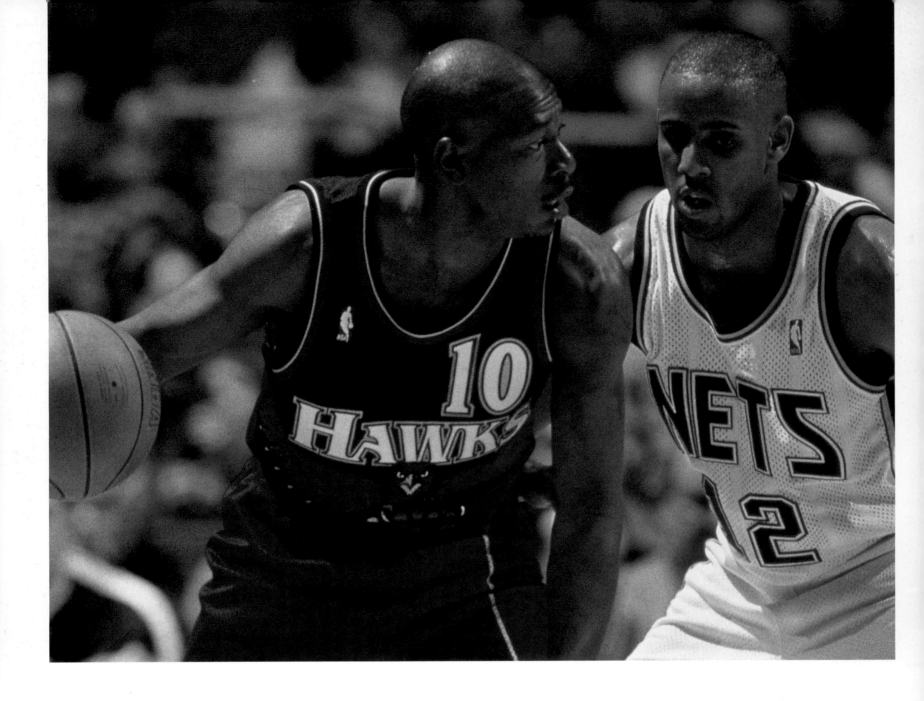

MOOKIE BLAYLOCK

Atlanta Hawks

$3,100,000   72=

Stat Attack   Career Highlights

Born:	March 20, 1967, Garland, TX	1989	Selected in the first round of the NBA Draft by the New Jersey Nets
Ht/Wt:	6—1, 185 pounds	1994	Played in his first career All-Star Game
School:	University of Oklahoma	1996	Established Hawks' single-season records for three-pointers made (231) and attempted (623)
Pro Career:	New Jersey Nets (1989–92), Atlanta Hawks (1992–)	1997	NBA leader in threes attempted (604) and finished second in threes made (221)
Career Avgs:	14.4 ppg, 4.3 rpg, 6.9 apg, 2.5 spg	1998	Led the league in steals for the second straight season with 2.61 spg

Mookie Blaylock may be the grittiest of NBA point guards. The man with the given name of Daron Oshay Blaylock is not going to fly through the air for a hoop and the next flashy pass he throws will be his first, but Blaylock is a very efficient player. Blaylock's greatest asset is his defense. Mookie has extra-quick hands, a muscular build and a willingness to get beat up a bit, all of which allows him to stifle almost any opposing point guard. Besides superior work on the defensive end, Blaylock has become an effective outside shooter. Once known as a guy you could leave alone behind the arc, Blaylock now consistently ranks among the league leaders in three-pointers. With a heady game that nicely complements his D and his shooting, Blaylock is indispensable. "Mookie is the catalyst of our team. When he's making things happen, we have a much better chance to win," say Hawks coach Lenny Wilkens.

Another fact about Mookie that many pop culture freaks out there should know: he is the favorite player of the members of Pearl Jam, and their album *Ten* was named in honor of his uniform number. Fascinating, huh?

Born:	March 28, 1971, Crenshaw, AL	**1994**	Selected by the Phoenix Suns in the first round of the NBA Draft
Ht/Wt:	6—6, 195 pounds	**1995**	Named to the NBA All-Rookie Second Team after leading the Suns in threes made (117) and attempted (313)
School:	Auburn University	**1995**	Won the NBA Three-Point Contest
Pro Career:	Phoenix Suns (1994–97), Cleveland Cavaliers (1997–)	**1997**	Named the NBA's Player of the Week after tallying 25.3 ppg, 5.7 rpg, 3.0 apg and 2.0 spg for the week ending 12/7/97
Career Avgs:	12.7 ppg, 3.6 rpg, 1.7 apg	**1998**	Teamed with the WNBA's Michelle Edwards to win the first All-Star 2ball competition during All-Star Weekend in New York

WESLEY PERSON

Cleveland Cavaliers

$3,000,900 — 74

Wesley Person and his brother, Chuck "The Rifleman" Person have a lot in common. They're both NBA swingmen who had outstanding college careers at Auburn University (located in their native state of Alabama) and own major range on their jumpshots that make them substantial three-point threats. There's one big difference, though. While Chuck may have the biggest mouth in the NBA, Wesley is quiet as a mouse. Even on the court WP is kinda tough to notice. But pay attention and you'll see a cat with a lot of skills.

Besides his sweet shooting ability, Person is a great defender and a good passer. Like the silence, these are also traits that brother Chuck does not possess in abundance. Regardless, it's still Wes's shot that gets him the attention: "Every time he shoots, you honestly think it's going to go in. You get that feel. That's the mark of a good shooter." These are the words of Person's former head coach, the experienced Mike Fratello.

Just don't expect Person to squawk about his skills. That's up to the other NBA player in the family.

Born:	December 19, 1964, Kaunas, Lithuania	1988	Won a gold medal with the Soviet Union at the 1988 Olympics
Ht/Wt:	7—3, 292 pounds	1995	Won the European Club Championship with Real Madrid of Spain and was named MVP of the European Final Four
School:	N/A		
Pro Career:	Portland Trailblazers (1995–)	1995	Selected with the 24th pick overall in the NBA Draft by the Portland Trailblazers
Career Avgs:	14.2 ppg, 8.5 rpg, 2.3 apg	1996	Named NBA Player of the Week after averaging 20.3 ppg, 9.5 rpg and 2.0 apg for the week ending March 31
		1997	Scored a career-high 33 points against the Dallas Mavericks
		1999	Reached the Western Conference Finals with the TrailBlazers

ARVYDAS SABONIS

Portland Trailblazers

$3,000,800   75=

There's a saying you'll occasionally hear on the TV highlight shows (ESPN's *Sportscenter*, to be specific) when they're showing an Arvydas Sabonis clip: "He's not My-vydas. He's not Your-vydas. He's Our-vydas." And aren't we lucky to have him.

After a lengthy career spent dominating the competition throughout Europe, Sabonis made his long-awaited NBA debut in '95 at the age of 30. Injuries and age had stolen many of the moves that made Sabonis somewhat of a worldwide legend in the late '80s and early '90s, but the man can still do some wondrous things. There's the slowly-developing hook shot: the 20-foot "jump" shot on which Sabonis barely leaves his feet and never misses; and last, but definitely not least, there's the passing. Sabonis was either born with or taught the way to find the open man; no NBA big man is better than Sabonis at hitting cutters, and he'll even do it with some flair. That's the main reason NBA fans are glad that he's "ours."

So are the TrailBlazers, according to coach Mike Dunleavy. "Our offense is based on unselfishness and sharing the ball. No one's better than Arvydas at doing that."

Born:	December 11, 1976, Marietta, GA	1996	Named Pac-10 Player of the Year Honors, the first freshman ever to be so named
Ht/Wt:	6—9, 230 pounds	1996	Selected third overall in the NBA Draft by the Vancouver Grizzlies
School:	University of California	1996	Selected as December Co-Rookie of the Month (with Kerry Kittles)
Pro Career:	Vancouver Grizzlies (1996–)	1997	Named February NBA Rookie of the Month
Career Avgs:	21.1 ppg, 7.1 rpg, 2.6 apg	1997	Netted 17 points during the NBA Rookie Game during All-Star Weekend
		1998	Led the Grizzlies in points and steals with 22.3 ppg and 1.09 spg, respectively

SHAREEF ABDUR-RAHIM

Vancouver Grizzlies

$3,000,800 75=

Shareef Abdur-Rahim can do most anything on a basketball court, and the thing he does best is score. Based on his scoring and all-around talents, Abdur-Rahim should be considered amongst the game's greats, but he is hampered by one not-so-minor problem. He plays in Vancouver.

Now Vancouver is a beautiful city, and 'Reef's game has certainly grown since he came into the league after just one year of college, but no one knows who he is. The Grizzlies get less media attention than any team in the league, and there are undoubtedly folks out there who call themselves basketball fans who wouldn't recognize Abdur-Rahim if he slapped them in the face. Nike has put Abdur-Rahim in a few TV ads, which always helps matters, and if the Grizz could pick up some veterans and maybe sniff a .500 season, then he may start to get some ink. To Abdur-Rahim's credit he hasn't bitched about the situation, and he signed the standard six-year, $71 million contract extension he was eligible for, which will kick in next year. Lucky Vancouver, says Grizzlies' head coach Brian Hill. "Shareef has a natural ability to put the ball in the basket, and what's amazing is that he's just scratching the surface. His best basketball is definitely ahead of him."

DANNY MANNING

Phoenix Suns

$3,000,000 | **77=**

Stat Attack | Career Highlights

Born:	May 17, 1966, Hattiesburg, MS
Ht/Wt:	6—10, 244 pounds
School:	University of Kansas
Pro Career:	Los Angeles Clippers (1988–1993), Atlanta Hawks (1994), Phoenix Suns (1994–)
Career Avgs:	16.6 ppg, 6.0 rpg, 2.8 apg

1988 Consensus National College Player of the Year, and National Champion after Kansas defeated Oklahoma for the NCAA Title

1988 Taken with the first overall pick in the NBA Draft by the Clippers

1993 Netted a career-high 43 points against the Chicago Bulls

1993 Recorded his first career triple-double against the Washington Bullets, scoring 12 points, grabbing 12 rebounds and handing out 12 assists

1994 Named to his second All-Star Game

1997 Scored his 10,000th career point

Danny Manning is a lifetime baller. As a high school senior, Manning was the nation's highest-rated high school player. Then Manning went to the University of Kansas, where he stayed four years and cappped one of the greatest all-around college careers in history with a National Championship win. Manning's rookie year got off to a good enough start, but within months of his career beginning Manning's devotion to the game was tested in a way he could never have imagined. Manning tore ligaments in his left knee and missed 10 months. He fought his way back from that knee injury, but in '95 Manning ripped up his other knee. Lesser men most definitely would have hung it up after Round Two under the knife, but Manning fought back again. Today, Manning's knees are a wreck and the rest of his body aches pretty bad as well, but he's still playing the game he loves. And playing it quite well.

"When I coached him, I thought he had the chance to be one of the great players ever," remembers college coach Larry Brown. "The knee injuries have obviously prevented a lot of that, but he has still had a great, great career."

Born:	March 25, 1965, New Orleans, LA
Ht/Wt:	5—11, 180 pounds
School:	University of S. California
Pro Career:	Seattle SuperSonics (1988–90), Denver Nuggets (1990–91), San Antonio Spurs (1992–93), Houston Rockets (1991–92), Spurs (1992–93), Golden State Warriors (1993–94), Spurs (1994–)
Career Avgs:	8.9 ppg, 1.8 rpg, 6.2 apg

1993	Named captain of the Golden State Warriors after playing just nine days with the team
1995	Increased his scoring average in his seven first seasons in the league
1997	Snapped a streak of 378 consecutive games played against the Boston Celtics on March 14
1997	Dished out a career-high 20 assists twice during the season
1998	Led the Spurs and ranked 11th overall in the league in assists with 7.9 apg
1999	Led the Spurs to the NBA Finals for the first time in franchise history

AVERY JOHNSON
San Antonio Spurs

$3,000,000   77=

The player-haters have been speaking to the Spurs for a long time now. "You can't do anything in the Playoffs with Avery Johnson at point guard," they say. "He's too short, and — damn, what is with that shot?"

Well, in '99 the haters got knocked for a loop. Look at the Spurs' dominant run to the NBA title and you'll see that the spearhead for their efforts is none other than Avery Johnson. Sure, Johnson is still short, and you wouldn't use his shot in an instructional video, but he's certainly learned how to win.

Johnson's secret is to play with emotion and to know where to go with the ball. Lucky for him, team-mates like David Robinson and Tim Duncan make those decisions pretty easy. Whether his game has really improved dramatically in the last few years or he's just playing with some great team-mates (the answer probably lies somewhere in between), respect has finally been given to Johnson, at least by his teammates: "We wouldn't be where we are if it wasn't for Avery," said Robinson during the Playoff run. "He's a key to our team."

Born:	June 30, 1965, Fort Lauderdale, FL	1988	Named NBA Rookie of the Year
		1988	Won the gold medal at the 1992 Olympic Games as a member of the "Dream Team"
Ht/Wt:	6—5, 220 pounds		
School:	Kansas State University	1993	Named to the All-NBA Second Team
		1995	Matched his career-high with 47 points against the Houston Rockets on December 15
Pro Career:	Golden State Warriors (1988–91), Sacramento Kings (1991–98), Washington Wizards (1999–)		
		1995	Named MVP of the All-Star Game after hitting for 23 points in 22 minutes
		1997	Set a new NBA record with six four-point plays
Career Avgs:	22.9 ppg, 4.2 rpg, 3.8 apg	1998	Named to his sixth consecutive All-Star Team
		1998	Finished the season with a 23.2 ppg average, becoming just the fourth player ever to average 20 ppg in each of his first 10 seasons

MITCH RICHMOND

Washington Wizards

$3,000,000 77=

When it comes to wins and dollars, Mitch Richmond has lost. Having spent a few mediocre years in Golden State followed by seven years in Sac-Town when the Kings stank and then finally an ugly '99 campaign with the Wizards, Richmond knows little about collecting W's.

Money-wise, no NBA players know what the word "suffer" means, but in relative terms Richmond has been hurt by his decision to sign a long-term deal with the Kings before contracts exploded. Rock finally has a chance to change that this summer as a free agent, and while he may not command what he could have two years ago you can expect Richmond to get a deal in the neighborhood of three years for $30 million, and you can be sure he's earned it.

But despite the preceding facts, Mitch Richmond is certainly no person to feel sorry for. He's had as prolific a career as most any two-guard not named Michael, and he's impressed team-mates and opponents in the process: "Mitch is really a professional, the type of guy you want to see win," says teammate Juwan Howard.

With a new contract and perhaps even a new team, it may finally happen for Mitch.

Born:	June 25, 1964, Harrisonburg, VA	1986	Selected in the first round of the NBA Draft by the Utah Jazz
Ht/Wt:	6—5, 205 pounds	1987	Had the first four-point play in Cleveland Cavaliers' history against the Washington Bullets
School:	Virginia Tech University	1993	Won the NBA's Sixth Man Award
Pro Career:	Utah Jazz (1986–87), Cleveland Cavaliers (1987–88), Charlotte Hornets (1988–98), Milwaukee Bucks (1998–)	1994	Set a new Hornets' record by connecting on 43 straight free-throws
		1994	Appeared in his second Three-Point Shootout during All-Star Weekend
		1996	Scored a career-high 38 points against the Toronto Raptors
Career Avgs:	12.8 ppg, 2.6 rpg, 1.9 apg	1997	Scored his 10,000th career point

DELL CURRY

Milwaukee Bucks

$3,000,000   77=

Throughout the '80s the Detroit Pistons had a special weapon. He may not have been as important as Isaiah Thomas or Bill Laimbeer, but Vinnie Johnson was still effective in his role as the "Microwave," a guy counted on for instant O off the bench. Consider Dell Curry the '90s Microwave.

After an excellent college career at Virginia Tech, Curry's pro career started slow; but when he was selected by the Charlotte Hornets in the Expansion Draft prior to the Hornets' inaugural season, he instantly became a key player. Like Johnson, Curry's specialty quickly became scoring points in a hurry, usually after not even starting the game. Curry could go to the basket, sure, but most of his damage has always come on jumpers, both from three-land and from about 18 feet away — a shot that few players even take anymore. Curry often did his damage in bunches, and he did it enough to leave Charlotte as the franchise's all-time leading scorer.

"What Dell did for us, in terms of coming off the bench and still being so productive, was very important to our team," says ex-Hornets coach Dave Cowens.

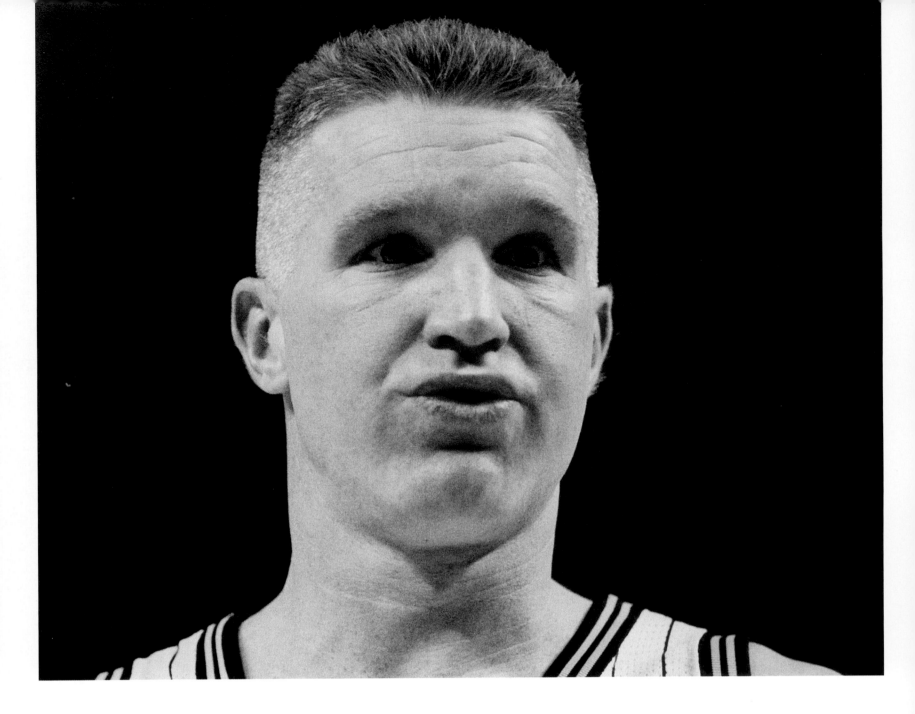

CHRIS MULLIN
Indiana Pacers

$2,940,000 | **81**

Stat Attack   Career Highlights

Born:	July 30, 1963, New York, NY	1985	Selected in the first round of the NBA Draft by the Golden State Warriors
Ht/Wt:	6—7, 215 pounds	1989	Tallied a career-high 47 points against the L.A. Clippers
School:	St. John's University	1990	Set a Warriors record by making 11 field goals without a miss
Pro Career:	Golden State Warriors (1985–97), Indiana Pacers (1997–)	1991	Named to the All-NBA First Team
		1992	Led the NBA in minutes played for the second straight year
Career Avgs:	19.1 ppg, 4.3 rpg, 3.7 apg, 1.6 spg	1992	Won a gold medal as a member of the "Dream Team" in 1992
		1993	Named an All-Star for the fifth time
		1998	Led the league in free-throw shooting

Without a doubt Chris Mullin is still an effective NBA player. Give him even an inch of space on the perimeter and he'll wet a jumper in your face. Look up from your dribble for a second and Mullin can still snatch the ball from you. Lose your man for a second on defense and you can bet Mullin will find him. And yet he is now a slow and unathletic man, capable of about 20 minutes a night.

There's nothing terribly wrong about the Mullin of today — just don't think you're seeing the real Chris Mullin. After a slow start to his NBA Career and before injuries started wracking his body in '93, Mullin enjoyed a four-year run during which he was the Western Conference's Larry Bird, destroying the competition as a high-scoring member of the Golden State Warriors.

After his Warriors career ran out of steam, Mullin was thrilled to be traded to the Pacers in the summer of '97, and the Pacers were equally happy to pick him up. A near-contemporary of Mullin is current Pacers coach Bird, and he sums up Mullin better than anyone else could: "He plays the game the way I liked to play."

STEPHON MARBURY
New Jersey Nets

$2,900,000 | **82=**

Kevin Garnett and Stephon Marbury were supposed to revolutionize the NBA, and for a while it looked like they would, as the two energetic and athletic cats spent over two seasons making Minneapolis's frigid winter nights seem warm. But while Marbury's alley played beautifully with KG's oop, Steph wasn't all that happy in Minny. So midway through the '99 season, Marbury and his agent forced the T-Wolves to trade their young point guard to the Nets.

New Jersey is a nice fit for Steph, and not just because it gave him the contract extension he wanted (six-year, $71 million package that is the standard max for his rookie class) but because NJ is close to home. Steph is a native New Yorker, and remains a hero throughout the metropolitan area, as any true NYC fan can rattle off a tale about Steph from his days as the city's most famous high school player. Now Steph's home, and the Nets are happy to have him. "Stephon is a great guy to play with since he's so quick, and he can run the offense so well. He's definitely one of, if not the, best point guards in the league" says Keith Van Horn. Remember the plans people had for Garnett and Marbury? Make that Van Horn and Marbury.

Stat Attack

Born:	February 20, 1977, New York, NY
Ht/Wt:	6—2, 180 pounds
School:	Georgia Tech University
Pro Career:	Minnesota Timberwolves (1996–99), New Jersey Nets (1999–)
Career Avgs:	17.9 ppg, 2.8 rpg, 8.4 apg

Career Highlights

1996	Selected by the Minnesota Timberwolves with the second pick overall in the NBA Draft
1996	Netted a rookie-season high of 33 points to go with eight assists against the Utah Jazz
1997	Named to the NBA All-Rookie First Team
1997	Led the Timberwolves to their first-ever Playoff appearance after his first season in the NBA
1998	Led the Timberwolves in assists with 8.6 apg, good enough for fourth in the league
1999	Traded to the Nets, one of his hometown teams

Born:	April 20, 1973, Pasadena, CA	**1994** Selected in the NBA Draft by the Los Angeles Clippers
Ht/Wt:	6—7, 236 pounds	**1995** Scored a rookie-season high of 30 points against the Phoenix Suns
School:	University of California	**1995** Finished second on the Clippers in scoring with 14.1 ppg
Pro Career:	Los Angeles Clippers (1994–)	**1997** Tallied a career-high 32 points against the Miami Heat
Career Avgs:	11.6 ppg, 4.2 rpg, 1.3 apg	**1998** Set career highs in scoring, field-goal percentage (.481), three-point percentage (.353), rebounds (6.1 rpg), assists (1.8 apg) and steals

LAMOND MURRAY

Los Angeles Clippers

$2,900,000   82=

Lamond Murray is the typical Clipper. He had a standout college career, entered the NBA as a high-draft pick and got thrown on a team that is loaded with guys like him. By '98, however, Murray had lifted himself above the morass that engulfs many Clippers and began to show some scoring skills that could one day make him a star.

Entering the '99 season, Murray began making noise about how he'd want out of LA when his contract expired after the season, so the Clips cut his minutes back a bit. But if they were trying to hurt Murray's earning power, it was too late; Lamond had already shown that he has the skills to start at the off-guard or small forward positions and hit double figures in points on a nightly basis. He could also come off the bench and provide O in a hurry.

"You've got to like Lamond's game, 'cause he can score on you off the dribble or with the jumper," says teammate Sherman Douglas.

Since Murray has understandably grown tired of life as a Clip, he's ready to move on. And plenty of other teams are ready to sign him.

BOBBY PHILLS
Charlotte Hornets

$2,900,000   82=

There's nothing glamorous about Hornets' off-guard Bobby Phills. About the best thing Phills brings to the court is a chiseled body: and a strong desire to help his team.

Phills' attitude stems from the fact that he knows how the other half lives. A collegiate star at the unrenowned Southern University, Phills didn't get drafted until midway through the second round, and then didn't even make it with the team the picked him (the Bucks). This dis led Phills to the CBA, where he busted his ass for a year before getting his chance with the Cavaliers. As a Cav, Phills showed a good work ethic and some phenomenal defensive skills.

Phills has continued to be an extremely selfless player with Charlotte, even moving to the small forward position this past season after Eddie Jones was brought to the Hive. At 6—5, Phills really has no business playing the three, but don't try to tell this guy he can't do something.

"It took Bobby a while to develop, and to get a chance in this league. You're not going to slow him down now," says ex-teammate Terrell Brandon.

Stat Attack   Career Highlights

Born:	December 20, 1969, Baton Rouge, LA	1991	Signed with the Cleveland Cavaliers after being named to the CBA All-Rookie Team
Ht/Wt:	6—5, 226 pounds	1994	Scored the first points at Gund Arena on a medium-range jumper against the Houston Rockets on November 8
School:	Southern University		
Pro Career:	Cleveland Cavaliers (1991–97), Charlotte Hornets (1997–)	1995	Tallied a career-high 43 points against the Portland TrailBlazers
		1996	Finished seventh in the league in three-point percentage, hitting on 44% of his long-range shots
Career Avgs:	10.9 ppg, 3.2 rpg, 2.7 apg	1996	Named to the NBA All-Defensive Second Team

Born:	December 31, 1970, San Bernadino, CA	1993	Drafted by the Utah Jazz in the first round of the NBA Draft
Ht/Wt:	6—7, 225 pounds	1993	Tallied seven points in the inaugural Rookie Game during All-Star Weekend
School:	Long Beach State University	1996	Netted a career-best 23 points against the TrailBlazers
Pro Career:	Utah Jazz (1993–)	1997	Set career highs in scoring (10.8 ppg), rebounding (4.1 rpg), assists (1.5 apg) and steals (1.59 spg)
Career Avgs:	7.5 ppg, 3.3 rpg, 1.0 apg	1998	Appeared in his second straight NBA Finals against the Chicago Bulls

BRYON RUSSELL
Utah Jazz

$2,800,000   85=

The Utah Jazz have to be the worst-named team in the NBA. Jazz, the funkiest, most soulful form of musical expression ever, and its namesake is some white-bread team that moved from New Orleans to Utah?! Well, at least Bryon Russell plays for the Jazz.

Russell brings some real ball to the staid fans of Utah, what with his high-flying dunks, ghetto-grimy defense and obvious enthusiasm for the game. The Jazz are also lucky to have him simply for the skills the man has. Russell owns a serviceable outside shot and he can D up on opponents of all shapes and sizes.

After a slow start to his career (perhaps caused by culture shock?) Russell has become a true player in the last few years, hitting big baskets and becoming one of Utah's go-to guys as the Jazz marched to the NBA Finals in back-to-back seasons. "Bryon is an important member of our team because he's willing to take on so many different jobs," says Jazz head coach Jerry Sloan.

And best of all, he does it all with a flair his teammates badly lack.

Born:	July 20, 1975, Merced, CA	1996	Selected fourth overall in the NBA Draft by the Milwaukee Bucks
Ht/Wt:	6—5, 205 pounds	1997	Named to the NBA All-Rookie Second Team
School:	University of Connecticut	1998	Netted a career-high 40 points to go along with 10 rebounds against the Minnesota Timberwolves
Pro Career:	Milwaukee Bucks (1996–)	1998	Finished in the top 20 in the league in free-throw percentage (.875), minutes played (40.1), threes made (134) and points scored (19.5 ppg)
Career Avgs:	16.6 ppg, 4.4 rpg, 3.5 apg	1999	Scored 20 or more points 13 times in the abbreviated season

RAY ALLEN

Milwaukee Bucks

$2,800,000   85=

Despite playing in the relative media vacuum that is Milwaukee, Wisconsin, Ray Allen has the potential to be one of the NBA's best-known players. Allen is a satin-smooth player, with plenty of sweet moves and slick jumping ability.

Perhaps most important in the image-conscious NBA, Allen has movie-star good looks which he's already used to his advantage. If anyone hadn't heard about Allen during his three-year stint at the University of Connecticut or when he wowed the NBA as a rookie with the Bucks, they certainly noticed Ray when he starred in Spike Lee's summer '98 hit *He Got Game*. Allen played high school hoops phenom Jesus Shuttlesworth in a move that also featured silver screen legend Denzel Washington and a host of other NBA players.

That movie introduced Allen to a whole new set of fans; and if they learned to watch him play because of it, all the better. "Ray's got it all; the looks, the charm and the game. He's gonna be a star into the next millennium," says Lee, himself a knowledgeable observer of the game.

Allen may even get people to pay attention to Milwaukee.

Born:	September 25, 1976, Denver, CO	1996	Drafted in the first round by the Boston Celtics
Ht/Wt:	6—3, 202 pounds	1997	Scored 15 points while handing out four assists in his NBA debut for the Celtics
School:	Colorado University	1997	Had a rookie season-high 27 points against the Vancouver Grizzlies
Pro Career:	Boston Celtics (1997–98), Toronto Raptors (1998), Denver Nuggets (1999–)	1998	Led all rookies in three-pointers made (107) and attempted (325) for the '97–98 season
Career Avgs:	12.1 ppg, 2.3 rpg, 3.9 apg	1999	Scored a career-high 32 points against the Seattle SuperSonics

CHAUNCEY BILLUPS

D e n v e r
N u g g e t s

$2,750,000   87

An undeserving victim of the impatience that many NBA executives suffer from, Chauncey Billups played the '99 season with his third team in just two seasons. And this guy was the third pick in the Draft!

Well, the teams that did give up on Billups (Boston and Toronto) are going to regret it, as Billups spent '99 showing everyone around the league why he was picked so high in the first place. Billups can play both guard positions smartly, and he has the athleticism to take the ball to the rim. And considering the kid only played two years of college ball, is it any surprise that he needed a year of seasoning to get things going?

Speaking of development, Billups' finest moments as a player have all come in or around Denver, so that was probably a factor in the overall play Billups showed as an NBA sophomore. Billups first made a name for himself as an All-American high school player in Denver, and then spent his brief college experience just half an hour away at Colorado University.

"Chauncey was happy to come home, and we're happy to have him. The Nuggets only expect Chauncey to get better in the next couple of seasons," says Nugs GM Dan Issel.

LOY VAUGHT
Detroit Pistons

$2,500,000 | **88**

For years an underappreciated workhorse for the Los Angeles Clippers, Loy Vaught jumped at his chance for free agency before the '99 season and headed back to his native Michigan to play for the Pistons. Vaught's story doesn't have a fairy-tale ending just yet, due to a bad back that hindered his first season in Motown from day one, but at least he's not with the Clippers anymore.

Vaught muscled his way into the nation's consciousness as the hard-working frontcourt member of a glossy University of Michigan team that won the '89 National Championship with offensive studs Glen Rice and Rumeal Robinson. Then it was on to to the other LA, where Vaught spent eight years as a sort of Charles Oakley West. The emphasis was on bullying people on the boards, and Vaught did it well enough to become the Clippers' all-time leading rebounder. But Vaught didn't simply rest on his laurels as a rebounder, instead picking up a highly-efficient 18-foot jump shot that the opposition had to respect.

"If Loy gets healthy, we're counting on him to hit that jumper and to get some boards. He'll be a key guy whether he starts or comes off the bench," says Pistons head coach Alvin Gentry.

Stat Attack

Born:	February 27, 1968, Grand Rapids, MI
Ht/Wt:	6—9, 240 pounds
School:	University of Michigan
Pro Career:	LA Clippers (1990–1998), Detroit Pistons (1999–)
Career Avgs:	11.3 ppg, 7.8 rpg, 1.0 apg

Career Highlights

1989	Won a National Championship as a member of the Michigan Wolverines
1990	Selected in the first round of the NBA Draft by the Clippers
1995	Scored a career-high 33 points against the Houston Rockets
1996	Led the Clippers with 49 double-doubles
1997	Named NBA Player of the Week after averaging 21.3 ppg and 11.3 rpg for the week ending March 3
1998	Became the Clippers' all-time leader in rebounds with 4, 471

Born:	August 23, 1978, Philadelphia, PA
Ht/Wt:	6—7, 215 pounds
School:	Lower Merion High School
Pro Career:	Los Angeles Lakers (1996–)
Career Avgs:	13.8 ppg, 3.2 rpg, 2.4 apg

1996	Consensus pick as National High School Player of the Year
1997	Made his NBA debut at the age of 18 years, two months and 11 days, becoming the youngest player ever to appear in an NBA game
1997	Scored a Rookie Game-record 31 points during All-Star Weekend
1998	Became the youngest starter in the All-Star Game in NBA history
1999	Scored a career-high 38 points against the Orlando Magic
1999	Led the Lakers in steals (1.44 spg) and finished second on team in scoring (19.9 ppg)

KOBE BRYANT

Los Angeles Lakers

$2,200,000   89

To see some of Kobe Bryant's moves is to see a young Michael Jordan. To hear some of the breathless NBA announcers scream about Bryant while he's in mid-air is to be reminded of a young Jordan. And to watch Kobe in all sorts of advertisements, from Sprite soda to Adidas shoes, is like watching a young Jordan pitching Air Jordans and Classic Coke. After three full seasons, however, Bryant shows a grasp of the game that reminds no one of Jordan, although he'll be getting paid like Jordan when his new contract kicks in next year. Still, KB continues to look for the highlight play rather than the smart play, and he sometimes seems more concerned with his own stats than with winning.

Of course, perhaps the warts on Bryant's game are to be expected; the kid did come straight from high school. And he did average almost 20 points a game last season. And he has been thrown right into a pressure-packed situation. Teammate Robert Horry is certainly feeling for KB: "He's got the whole world in his hands with his game. He can already do everything, and he's still learning, which is bad news for his opponents. He's gonna be one of the all-time greats."

Maybe even the Air Apparent.

Born:	January 26, 1977, Daytona Beach, FL	1995	Member of the USA Basketball Junior National Team that played in the World Championships
Ht/Wt:	6—7, 215 pounds	1998	Reached the NCAA Final Four and received first-team All-ACC honors after his junior season at North Carolina
School:	University of North Carolina		
Pro Career:	Toronto Raptors (1999–)	1998	Drafted fifth overall by the Golden State Warriors, then traded immediately to the Toronto Raptors
Career Avgs:	18.3 ppg, 5.7 rpg, 3.0 apg	1999	Became the first player in Raptors' franchise history to be named Player of the Week after averaging 20 ppg, 7 rpg, and 1.6 bpg during the week ending March 21
		1999	Named NBA Rookie of the Year

VINCE CARTER
Toronto Raptors

$2,100,000   90

Even the NBA's staunchest supporter would admit that the '99 season, from its delayed beginning to its miserable scoring displays, was one of the worst in years. But even the NBA's biggest critic should realize that rookie Vince Carter is a guy that could turn things around.

Carter waltzed (or more accurately, glided), to the NBA's Rookie of the Year award, thanks to a season that saw him do a little bit of everything. Oh, there was the "Did you just see that?" type of dunk running across the TV screen every night of the season, but Carter did so much more than just provide fans with a cheap thrill. The hysteria that Toronto natives labeled "Vince-anity" also included a nice jump shot and more than 1.5 bpg, best among the rookies and remarkable for a guy that stands 6—7. Carter also made waves off the court, earning a fat endorsement deal with Puma, a shoe company that hadn't made any noise since Isaiah Thomas rocked 'em back in the day.

But it all came back to his play, which helped the Raptors make a run at their first Playoff appearance in franchise history; "The kid is the truth. Offense, defense and a great attitude," says Toronto coach Butch Carter.

Born:	November 27, 1971, Kenosha, WI	1994	Named to the NBA All-Rookie Second Team
Ht/Wt:	6—1, 190 pounds	1995	Established Lakers franchise highs in three-pointers made (183) and attempted (511) in a season
School:	University of Cincinnati	1998	Selected to his first career All-Star Game
Pro Career:	Los Angeles Lakers (1993–98), Denver Nuggets (1999–)	1998	Led the Lakers in assists and three-pointers for the fifth consecutive season
Career Avgs:	15.1 ppg, 2.7 rpg, 7.3 apg	1999	Scored a career-high 41 points against his former team, the Lakers

NICK VAN EXEL

Denver Nuggets

$1,900,000   91=

Despite a high-profile college career at Cincinnati, Nick Van Exel was still not very respected as he entered the NBA Draft, and slipped all the way until the 37th pick before getting scooped up by the Lakers.

Rather than be discouraged, however, the scowling Van Exe. used the draft snub as motivation to show doubting teams around the league that he belonged. It didn't take him long. Van Exel started as a rook, and in year two was the sparkplug on a Lakers team that shocked the Sonics in the first round of the Playoffs. Besides solid point play, Van Exel made his mark with his long-range bombing as the left-hander showed an uncanny ability to hit clutch shots.

Van Exel and the Lakers had soured on each other by the end of '98, and so he was sent to Denver. NVE responded by scoring 16.5 ppg and showed that he'd retained his flair for the dramatic when he dropped a career-high 41 points on the heads of his former teammates in a late-season game. He's a free agent in '99, but all indications are that Nick will remain with the Nuggets. "We want Nick with this franchise for a long time. He's a point guard that we can count on," says Denver GM Dan Issel.

JASON WILLIAMS
Sacramento Kings

$1,900,000 91=

In a lockout-shortened '99 season, no player gave fans more reason to keep the faith in the game they love than mind-bending rookie point guard Jason Williams. Thanks to a past littered with minor legal incidents, Williams entered the '98 Draft an unknown quantity; he'd been kicked off the University of Florida team in the middle of his senior season, so who could trust him?

Well, the historically-jinxed Sacramento Kings took a gamble, and JWill paid them back tenfold. With lightning quickness, radar-like range on his three-pointers and a flair that hadn't been seen since Maravich was around, Williams was the talk of the '99 Season. Williams started every game of the season at point guard and did it with grace, running the show for a Kings team that had its best season since the mid-'80s.

The winning of games, combined with the winning-over of fans, impressed anyone who watched. "When I first saw him, I said 'Pistol Pete'," says Boston Celtics guard Bruce Bowen. "He has that knack for the game that Maravich, Bird, Magic Johnson had; you can't teach what he has."

Stat Attack

Born:	November 18, 1975, Belle, WV
Ht/Wt:	6—1, 190 pounds
School:	University of Florida
Pro Career:	Sacramento Kings (1999–)
Career Avgs:	12.8 ppg, 3.1 rpg, 6.0 apg

Career Highlights

1998	Was leading Florida in scoring (17.1 ppg) and assists (6.7apg) when he was dismissed from the team
1998	Drafted seventh overall in the NBA Draft
1999	Scored 21 points and grabbed five steals in his first-ever NBA game
1999	Led all rookies in three-pointers made and attempted
1999	Finished second in the NBA Rookie of the Year Voting

PAUL PIERCE
Boston Celtics

$1,800,000 | 93

Born:	October 13, 1977, Oakland, CA	**1997** Named MVP of the Big 12 Conference Tournament for the first of two consecutive years
Ht/Wt:	6—7, 220 pounds	**1998** Consensus First Team All-American after his junior year at Kansas
School:	University of Kansas	**1999** Named NBA Rookie of the Month for February after leading all rookies with 20.4 ppg, and the entire NBA with 2.73 spg
Pro Career:	Boston Celtics (1999–)	
Career Avgs:	16.5 ppg, 6.4 rpg, 2.4 apg	**1999** Named to the NBA All-Rookie First Team
		1999 Named *SLAM* magazine's NBA Rookie of the Year

The least ballyhooed of the NBA's latest rookie class when the season ended, Celtics' do-everything forward Paul Pierce may turn out to be the best of the bunch. Of course, heading into the NBA Draft, that's what many people would have expected. Here was a guy who had played three (a near-eternity in this day and age) solid years at Kansas, owned all the requisite skills for a long and prosperous NBA career, and entered the Draft expected to be picked no lower than four. Pierce went 10th.

He instantly started to do his thing, which can be explained like this: minimal flash and maximum substance, with an efficiency to everything the swingman does. If he was going to take a long jumper, he made it a triple. If he got a defensive rebound, he turned it into a fast break. "Paul Pierce is the best rookie in the NBA," said Nets forward Kendall Gill during the season. "He brings everything. A total player. He plays defense, he can score, he makes big plays. Pierce is a complete player that plays like a veteran."

What were those nine stupid teams thinking?

JOE SMITH
Minnesota Timberwolves

$1,750,000 94=

I n 1999, Joe Smith proved yet again that he is no "Ordinary" Joe. The first pick in the 1995 Draft and a one-time rising star with Golden State, by the end of the 1998 season Smith was being written off as a "has-been." Smith still had physical tools, but he was no longer putting up good numbers. However, signed as a bargain-basement free agent by the Timberwolves prior to the '99 season, Smith teamed with his good buddy Kevin Garnett to form one of the NBA's finest forward combos.

Smith made his impact felt both on offense, where he sports a pillowy-soft jumper as well as the ability to take the ball strong to the hoop, and on defense, where he blocked almost two shots per game. Smith's renewed efforts landed him among the top vote-getters for the NBA's Most Improved Player award. "Ever since we entered the draft together, we talked about how great it would be to play together," says Smith's slightly-richer teammate Kevin Garnett. "When I found out we had a chance to get him, I couldn't believe it. I was as happy as anyone. I had always thought we could be great playing together." He was right about that.

Stat Attack

Born:	July 26, 1975, Norfolk, VA
Ht/Wt:	6—10, 225 pounds
School:	University of Maryland
Pro Career:	Golden State Warriors (1995–98), Philadelphia 76ers (1998), Minnesota Timberwolves (1999–)
Career Avgs:	15.8 ppg, 7.8 rpg, 1.3 apg

Career Highlights

1995 Given the James A. Naismith Award as the College Player of the Year

1995 Picked first overall in the NBA Draft after two All-American seasons at the University of Maryland

1996 Scored a game-high 20 points in the Rookie All-Star Game in San Antonio

1996 Named to the NBA All-Rookie First Team

1999 Picked up both his 2,000th career rebound and 4,000th career point while playing for the Timberwolves

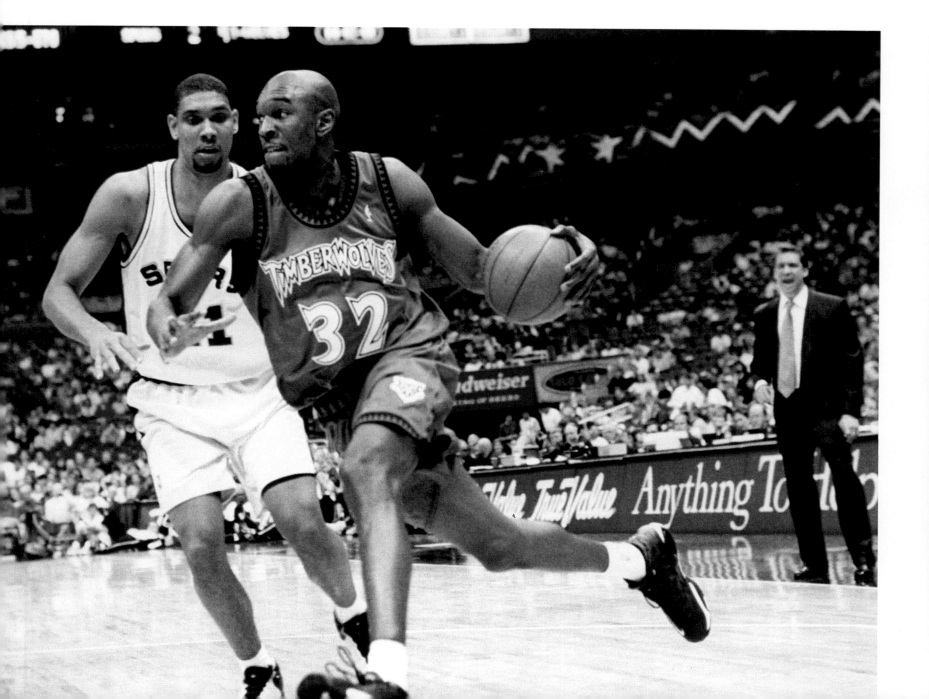

Born:	May 5, 1970, East St. Louis, IL	1993	Drafted in the first round by the Denver Nuggets
Ht/Wt:	6—8, 240 pounds	1993	Named to the NBA All-Rookie First Team after scoring a Nuggets rookie-record 1,205 points
School:	Notre Dame		
Pro Career:	Denver Nuggets (1992–98), Atlanta Hawks (1999)	1994	Grabbed a career-high 19 rebounds against the Rockets
		1997	Scored a career-high 39 points against the TrailBlazers
Career Avgs:	14.9 ppg, 7.7 rpg, 2.1 apg	1999	Scored 14 points in his debut with the Hawks

LAPHONSO ELLIS

Atlanta Hawks

$1,750,000   94=

The '99 season served as a perfect metaphor for LaPhonso Ellis's career. Signed as a free agent by the Atlanta Hawks to provide some scoring for Atlanta's usually punchless offense, Ellis did just that. Until he got hurt.

Offense and injuries have been the staples of Ellis's career ever since he entered the league after a terrific career at Notre Dame. Ellis had two awesome seasons to begin his career (14.7 and 15.4 ppg, respectively), then played all of six games in year three. The '96–97 season may have been Ellis's most frustrating, as the combo forward was averaging a career-high 21.9 ppg when he went down.

In '99, Ellis was averaging a respectable 11 points a night and giving the Hawks' bland offense a little flavor when the injury bug struck again. Ellis was lost for the season to a hernia after just 20 games. The absence of Ellis was felt often by the Hawks. "You can tell what we miss when we don't have LaPhonso," says Hawks coach Lenny Wilkens. "He's a guy that you can give the ball to in the post, and good things will happen."

If he stays healthy next season, they will.

Born:	October 30, 1976, Detroit, MI	1997	Left Michigan ranked 20th in career points (1,254) and rebounds (588)
Ht/Wt:	6—9, 260 pounds	1997	Drafted in the first round by the Clippers
School:	University of Michigan	1998	Selected to the NBA All-Rookie Second Team
Pro Career:	Los Angeles Clippers (1997–)	1999	Scored 14 consecutive fourth-quarter points in a Clippers win over the TrailBlazers
Career Avgs:	13.6 ppg, 4.6 rpg, 1.0 apg	1999	Scored a career-high 29 points against the Grizzlies

MAURICE TAYLOR

Los Angeles Clippers

$1,700,000   96

Seen as unfit for the pro game when he left the University of Michigan after three enigmatic seasons, Maurice Taylor has nonetheless used his wonderful skills to tap into his potential and become a solid NBA player.

Taylor may be just two years into his pro career — and with the hapless Clippers to boot — but he is already making it clear that he will be a force to be reckoned with. The '99 season saw Taylor average almost 17 points a night, and those are digits that cannot be ignored. Taylor's reasons have to begin with his physique and athleticism. Despite standing a fully-developed 6—9 and 260 pounds, Taylor can jump like a man that carries around 50 pounds fewer. The combination of hops and build allows Mo to throw down dunks with authority, while a feathery touch with his shot has led to Taylor's high scoring average.

So now a man that many scouts laughed at for leaving school early is working on a potential All-Star career. One guy who never slept on Taylor was his former college coach, Steve Fisher: "The people that doubted him had probably never seen him play. You have to watch Maurice to really appreciate all he can do."

OLDEN POLYNICE

Seattle SuperSonics

$1,000,000 | 97=

Stat Attack

Born:	November 21, 1964, Haiti	1987	Made his NBA debut after spending a year playing in Italy
Ht./Wt:	7—0, 250 pounds	1991	Scored a career-high 30 points against the Nuggets
School:	University of Virginia	1994	Scored 23 points and pulled down 21 rebounds — including a Kings-record 14 offensive boards — against the Bucks
Pro Career:	Seattle SuperSonics (1987–1990), LA Clippers (1990–92), Detroit Pistons (1992–93), Sacramento Kings (1993–98), Sonics (1999–)	1998	Picked up his 450th career block against the Celtics
		1999	Put up 11 points and 13 rebounds in his first game back with the Sonics
Career Avgs:	8.3 ppg, 7.0 rpg, 0.8 apg		

Career Highlights

Olden Polynice has been around the NBA for years thanks to a wide body, a strong work ethic and a great personality. OP spent this last season as a complementary player for the SuperSonics, doing what he could as a big man that rarely saw the ball.

Not that Polynice struggled with the reduced role; the man did grab 8.9 rpg, and he has handled loads of roles in the NBA. Furthermore, he's done it all while maintaining a wide grin and amusing players and reporters around the league with his unique sense of humor.

The varieties of on-court jobs that have been assigned to Polynice are a result of his "tweener" build and warrior-like mentality. Though Polynice may stand 7—0, at 250 he is often too small to guard some of the post powers that control the paint, yet is a tad slow and unrefined to play far forward. So OP has been shuffling between forward and center for the past 12 seasons, sacrificing his body and fighting for rebounds. The efforts haven't gone unnoticed. "Olden always practiced and played extremely hard for us. That's why he's remained an effective player for so long," says ex-Kings coach Eddie Jordan.

SAM PERKINS
Indiana Pacers

$1,000,000 97=

The 1982 UNC NCAA Championship team included Michael Jordan, James Worthy and Sam Perkins. Only one of them is still around, and that's Perkins, affectionately known around the league as "Sleepy Sam," "Sammy Smooth" or just plain "Smooth." Perkins earned the moniker with his laid-back nature, always-chill hairstyles (he's sported an afro, dreadlocks and corn rows in the past three years alone), and eyes that forever seem half-shut. Not that Perkins' offensive game is rough. Willing to bang and bruise on the defensive end, "Smooth" plays offense on the perimeter, specializing in three-pointers, an unbelievable rarity for a cat that plays center. And when he gets off one of his long-range bombs, it usually goes down the same way — smooth.

During his Carolina, Mavericks, and Lakers days, Perkins was more than a defender and three-point shooter, averaging 13-plus a night for eight straight seasons with a diverse offensive game. But in past seasons, as Perkins chases a championship, he's wisened up. "Sam isn't going to try and do something he can't. He knows what he's good at, and that's what he focuses on," says teammate Mark Jackson. That explains the duration of Smooth's career.

Stat Attack

Born:	June 14, 1961, Brooklyn, NY
Ht/Wt:	6—9, 260 pounds
School:	University of North Carolina
Pro Career:	Dallas Mavericks (1984–90), Los Angeles Lakers (1990–93), Seattle SuperSonics (1993–98), Indiana Pacers (1999)
Career Avgs:	12.7 ppg, 6.3 rpg, 1.6 apg

Career Highlights

1982	Won a National Championship with North Carolina
1984	Co-captain of the gold medal-winning US Olympic Team
1984	Drafted fourth overall by the Mavericks
1986	Recorded the only 30–20 game in Mavericks' history, collecting 31 points and 20 boards against the Houston Rockets
1991	Appeared in the NBA Finals with the Lakers, losing to the Bulls
1996	Appeared in the NBA Finals with the Sonics, losing to the Bulls
1997	Participated in the Three-Point Contest during All-Star Weekend

CHARLES BARKLEY
Houston Rockets

$1,000,000   97=

Career Highlights

1985	Named to the NBA All-Rookie Team
1988	Averaged a career-best 28.3 ppg
1991	Named NBA All-Star Game MVP after scoring 17 points and 22 rebounds
1992	Won an Olympic gold medal
1993	Won the NBA MVP Award
1993	Reached the Finals for the first and only time in his career
1995	Named to the NBA All-First Team
1998	Appeared in his 1,000th career game
1999	Joined Wilt Chamberlain as the only players in NBA history to top 23,000 points, 12,000 rebounds and 4,000 assists

If you look at this from the admittedly skewed world of professional sports, it's a shame that Charles Barkley made only the veteran's minimum salary in '99. But the fact that this sure-fire Hall of Famer and one of the most unique talents in NBA history did play for such a relatively small chunk of change speaks volumes about what matters to the man — winning a ring.

Despite the jaw-dropping scoring and rebounding digits that Barkley has put up for years, he has never won an NBA Title and that is all that keeps him going. Before the '99 campaign began, Barkley took the minimum so that the Rockets could sign Scottie Pippen and his six rings to an expensive long-term deal. The thinking by Barkley (and plenty of observers) was that with Barkley, Pippen and Hakeem Olajuwon all on the floor together, a title was a realistic goal. Instead, the top 50 triumvirate struggled, and Barkley ended yet another season as one of the greatest players ever not to win a championship. "It's a shame that we couldn't get Charles a title," said Pippen. "After all he's accomplished in this league, he certainly deserves it."

Stat Attack	Career Highlights

Born:	May 13, 1961, Trenton, NJ	1986	Named first-team NAIA for the third straight season while playing for tiny Southeastern Oklahoma State
Ht/Wt:	6—8, 220	1986	Drafted by the Detroit Pistons
School:	Southeastern Oklahoma State	1990	Won his second straight NBA Title as a member of the Detroit Pistons "Bad Boys"
Pro Career:	Detroit Pistons (1986–92), San Antonio Spurs (1993–95), Chicago Bulls (1995–98), Los Angeles Lakers (1999), who knows?	1991	Named NBA Defensive Player of the Year for the second straight season
		1992	Named to his second career All-Star Team
Career Avgs:	7.5 ppg, 12.8 rpg, 1.6 apg	1998	Won his third straight NBA Title as a member of the Chicago Bulls; after the '97 title he'd become the only player in NBA history to win back-to-back titles with two different teams

DENNIS RODMAN

Los Angeles Lakers

$1,000,000   97=

Dennis Rodman may not technically be an NBA player at the moment, but it seems highly likely that the tattooed and eccentric Rodman will return to the NBA next season. For one thing, former Bulls coach Phil Jackson, of whom Rodman is very fond, is probably going to be back in the league next year. And more fundamentally Rodman needs basketball and it kind of needs him too.

He needs the game because it pays him lots of money, gives him a stage on which to perform and gives him something to do when he isn't gambling or wrestling. The NBA needs him because it's populated with too many automata: look-alike, play-alike, sound-alike individuals who do little to spice up your evening if you're watching them play. "The Worm" does not have that problem. He also just happens to be one of the greatest rebounders in NBA history, as he's used a long body, quickness and all-out desire to pass 11,000 boards in his storied career.

When his most recent stint in pro hoops — with the Lakers — ended this past spring, L.A. center Shaquille O'Neal was sad to see him go: "He's the only one I've ever seen rebound in practice. And he played hard in games. He rebounded and set picks and played defense. If he comes to play, then who cares what he does off the court?"

1	Kevin Garnett	Timberwolves	$21,000,000
2	Patrick Ewing	Knicks	$17,000,000
3	Shaquille O'Neal	Lakers	$15,000,000
4	David Robinson	Spurs	$14,800,000
5	Shawn Kemp	Cavaliers	$14,280,000
=6	Scottie Pippen	Rockets	$14,000,000
	Horace Grant	Magic	$14,000,000
=8	Alonzo Mourning	Heat	$12,000,000
	Juwan Howard	Wizards	$12,000,000
10	Hakeem Olajuwon	Rockets	$11,600,000
11	Dikembe Mutombo	Hawks	$11,400,000
12	Antonio McDeyess	Nuggets	$11,250,000
13	Gary Payton	Sonics	$10,510,000
=14	Rod Strickland	Wizards	$10,000,000
	Charles Oakley	Raptors	$10,000.000
	Rik Smits	Pacers	$10,000,000
	Vlade Divac	Kings	$10,000,000
	Chris Webber	Kings	$10,000,000
19	Tom Gugliotta	Suns	$9,750,000
20	Reggie Miller	Pacers	$9,000,000

The Top-100 list

21	Anfernee Hardaway	Magic	$8,500,000		Kendall Gill	Nets	$4,400,000	=75	Arvydas Sabonis	Trailblazers	$3,000,800
22	Larry Johnson	Knicks	$8,460,000		Otis Thorpe	Wizards	$4,400,000		Shareef Abdur-Rahim	Grizzlies	$3,000,000
=23	Michael Finley	Mavericks	$8,000,000	50	Vin Baker	SuperSonics	$4,300,000	=77	Danny Manning	Suns	$3,000,000
	Allan Houston	Knicks	$8,000,000	51	Isaiah Rider	TrailBlazers	$4,210,000		Avery Johnson	Spurs	$3,000,000
	Latrell Sprewell	Knicks	$8,000,000	52	Darrell Armstrong	Magic	$4,200,000		Mitch Richmond	Wizards	$3,000,000
=26	Kenny Anderson	Celtics	$7,000,000	53	Tyrone Hill	76ers	$4,110,000		Dell Curry	Bucks	$3,000,000
	Elden Campbell	Hornets	$7,000,000	=54	John Stockton	Jazz	$4,000,000	81	Chris Mullin	Pacers	$2,940,000
28	Derrick Coleman	Hornets	$7,000,000		David Wesley	Hornets	$4,000,000	=82	Stephon Marbury	Nets	$2,900,000
29	Glenn Robinson	Bucks	$6,800,000		Chris Childs	Knicks	$4,000,000		Lamond Murray	Clippers	$2,900,000
30	Nick Anderson	Magic	$6,700,000		Dale Davis	Pacers	$4,000,000		Bobby Phills	Hornets	$2,900,000
31	Grant Hill	Pistons	$6,500,000		P.J. Brown	Heat	$4,000,000	=85	Bryon Russell	Jazz	$2,800,000
32	Karl Malone	Jazz	$6,100,000	59	Donyell Marshall	Warriors	$3,990,000		Ray Allen	Bucks	$2,800,000
=33	Eddie Jones	Hornets	$6,000,000	=60	Walt Williams	Trailblazers	$3,750,000	87	Chauncey Billups	Nuggets	$2,750,000
	Jason Kidd	Suns	$6,000,000		Clifford Robinson	Suns	$3,750,000	88	Loy Vaught	Pistons	$2,500,000
	Robert Horry	Lakers	$6,000,000	62	Derrick McKey	Pacers	$3,600,000	89	Kobe Bryant	Lakers	$2,200,000
35	Shawn Bradley	Mavericks	$5,940,000	=63	Jeff Hornacek	Jazz	$3,500,000	90	Vince Carter	Raptors	$2,100,000
=37	Steve Smith	Hawks	$5,400,000		Christian Laettner	Pistons	$3,500,000	=91	Nick van Exel	Nuggets	$1,900,000
	Glen Rice	Lakers	$5,400,000		Dee Brown	Raptors	$3,500,000		Jason Williams	Kings	$1,900,000
=39	Sean Elliott	Spurs	$5,330,000	66	Anthony Mason	Hornets	£3,470,000	93	Paul Pierce	Celtics	$1,800,000
	Ron Harper	Bulls	$5,300,000	67	Dana Barros	Celtics	$3,400,000	=94	Joe Smith	Timberwolves	$1,750,000
41	John Starks	Warriors	$5,100,000	=68	Detlef Schrempf	SuperSonics	$3,300,000		Laphonso Ellis	Hawks	$1,750,000
=42	Antonio Davis	Pacers	$5,000,000		Tim Duncan	Spurs	$3,300,000	96	Maurice Taylor	Clippers	$1,700,000
	Brian Grant	Blazers	$5,000,000	70	Mark Jackson	Pacers	$3,200,000	=97	Olden Polynice	Sonics	$1,000,000
44	Tim Hardaway	Heat	£4,800,000	71	Allen Iverson	76ers	$3,130,000		Sam Perkins	Pacers	$1,000,000
45	Doug Christie	Raptors	$4,750,000	=72	Keith van Horn	Nets	$3,100,000		Charles Barkley	Rockets	$1,000,000
46	Toni Kukoc	Bulls	$4,560,000		Mookie Blaylock	Hawks	$3,100,000		Dennis Rodman	Lakers	$1,000,000
=47	Jamal Mashburn	Heat	$4,400,000	74	Wesley Person	Cavaliers	$3,000,900				

The publishers would like to thank the following sources for their kind permission to reproduce the pictures in this book:

Allsport UK Ltd. 50/Brian Bahr 3r,tl, 46, 47, 76, 77, 127, 146, Al Bello 3bl, 31, 94, 104, 132, 134, 141, Jonathan Daniel 30, 40, 57, 66, 67, 69, 89, 101, 111, 128, 129, Stephen Dunn 2r, 16, 17, 29, 32, 80, 81, 82, 110, 153, Otto Greule 34, 44, 61, 95, 108, 109, 137, 152, Elsa Hasch 22, 78, 150, Tom Hauck 143, Harry How 15, 35, 53, Jed Jacobsohn 54, 72, 113, 145, Craig Jones 64, 125, Vincent Laforet 9, 18, 48, 49, 55, 84, Andy Lyons 27, 51, 70, 74, 75, 96, 115, 122, 139, Donald Miralle 156, Doug Pensinger 19, 25, 26, 36, 37, 38, 39, 45, 71, 97, 98, 99, 102, 106, 107, 112, 116, 117, 124, 126, 130, 138, 149, 151, Eliot Schecter 24, Ezra Shaw 2l, 12, 131, 133, Jamie Squire 21, 52, Matthew Stockman 83, 140, 157, David Taylor 4, 8, 13, Peter Taylor 41, 103, Todd Warshaw 5, 10, 11, 14, 20, 28, 73, 79, 85, 91, 119, 120, 136, 144, 148, 158, 159, Aubrey Washington 88
AP Photo 6, 7, 58, 62, 65, 68, 87, 92, 100, 142/Victoria Arocho 42, Duane Burleson 147, 123, Chuck Burton 63, 114, Michael Conroy 121, Chris Gardner 93, Morry Gash 59, Bill Kostroun 105, Alan Mothner 154, Rich Pedroncelli 118, Douglas C. Pizac 86, Nick Procaylo 135, Jim Rogash 60, Tom Strattman 23, David Zalubowski 33, 43, 90, 155
Corbis 56

Every effort has been made to acknowledge correctly and contact the source and/or copyright holder of each picture, and Carlton Books Limited apologises for any unintentional errors or omissions which will be corrected in future editions of this book.